# MOM MENTOR

## What Other Moms Never Told Me

*Written by Sabrina Schlesinger, Sarah Wood,
Melissa Miller, Diane Hwang, Lisa Hamel,
Kami Zumwalt, Rhonda Ihrig, Chris Blue,
Kyleen Baptiste, and Christi Stone.*

Mom Mentor: What Other Moms Never Told Me

# MOM MENTOR:
## WHAT OTHER MOMS NEVER TOLD ME

"Let's face it. MOM work is HARD work. Navigating the demands of parenthood, wifehood, and one's personhood, often leaves moms feeling underprepared and overwhelmed. Every mom needs a little encouragement. Every mom needs a little advice from time to time. Thankfully, the Mom Mentor Book provides the perfect blend of laughter, wisdom, and practical advice to help every mom gain strength and perspective at one of the most challenging but one of the most rewarding jobs ever created ... MOTHERHOOD!"

Julie Gorman

Founder of Restore Family & Married for a Purpose, Author of *What I Wish My Mother Told Me About Men*, *What I Wish My Mother Told Me About Marriage*, and *Married for a Purpose*.

OTHER MOMS
NEVER TOLD ME
I COULD NEVER GO
TO THE BATHROOM
AGAIN IN PRIVACY.

# A Note to The Reader

I was 8 months pregnant with my first child, sitting in a waiting room at the hospital when an older gentleman sat across from me. He smiles. I smiled. And then he began to share with me his unsolicited opinion and advice about whether or not I should use drugs while giving birth. Ummmmmm. Thanks, but no thanks. I would have answered to any name the nurse called to remove myself from that annoying encounter. I'm sure he meant well, but hello, cue the eye rolling emoji!

Helpful parenting advice finds us naturally from friends and family. We receive tidbits of wisdom at baby showers, while we are out and about with friends, from our mentors, and most of all, our own mothers. But sometimes, even with all the wisdom and advice thrown our way, we can still find ourselves in the middle of motherhood having absolutely no clue how to navigate the storm we are in or how to climb the mountain in front of us.

We are moms, all from different walks of life, with diverse experiences, coming together and sharing with you the advice we wished we would have received before becoming a mom.

The not-so-popular advice.

The embarrassing things no one wants to admit or talk about.

The behind-the-scenes ugly we don't advertise on social media.

Laugh with us and cry with us. But most of all, grow with us as we show you what is behind the curtain of our mothering with the hope that it will speak life, encouragement and offer you steps to get through it if you ever find yourself in a similar situation.

And the best compliment you could give us is to pass this book along to another mom who needs some love, care, wisdom, understanding and attention.

We hope you enjoy learning from our mistakes and gleaning from our victories.

Love + Blessings,
Sabrina Schlesinger
Founder of Mom Mentor
**www.MomMentor.org**

# Table of Contents

Other Moms Never Told Me ...

OTHER MOMS
NEVER TOLD ME
I WOULD HAVE TO
WEAR FISHNET
GRANDMA
PANTIES AFTER
GIVING BIRTH.

# Chapter 1

# Other Moms Never Told Me ...
# About the Loneliness I Would Battle

BY SABRINA SCHLESINGER

*"God sets the lonely in families,*
*He leads out the prisoners with singing;"*
*Psalm 68:6 NIV*

## I Didn't See That Coming:

I scrolled through their feed and saw all of their fun get togethers, ladies' nights out, and girlfriend weekends and wondered, "Why am I never invited to the party?" Was I jealous? Totally! But the jealousy I experienced was only a surface emotion. What was being uncovered was something far deeper.

If I'm honest, the real questions I was asking, but afraid to admit or verbalize was "Am I boring? Unlikeable? Forgettable?" I vividly remember thinking, "When will someone love me like I love them?" And I am not talking about spouses, because that's an entirely different chapter. I mean, have you ever known you are way more into your friend than they are into you? They are "your person" but you are pretty sure you aren't theirs. Depressing right? I wondered; will I ever have that kind of friendship I see so many other women seem to have? A true sisterhood. A Cristina to my Meredith. A Laverne to my Shirley. A Diana to my Anne. A Sookie to my Lorelai. (If you get any of these references, you are my people!)

Making friends came easy…when I was in elementary school. All I had to do was bump into you and you were my best friend. My childhood BFF was amazing. She had this beautiful long, blonde hair, and we were dance partners. Around Jr. High, my family moved to another state, and it was still relatively easy to make friends. My next best friend's name was Lisa…well, it's still her name! She is also writing a chapter in this book! She and I did everything together from Jr. High all the way until we graduated High School. She and her family were an answer to prayer.

And then I graduated.

And got married.

And moved to a new state.

And seven months later we moved again.

And then I got pregnant.

None of those things were bad, in fact they were all good, God moves. But I discovered because of life and circumstances, I was all alone in terms of friendship, and they didn't seem to come as easy as before. Can you relate?

Everyone had their own marriage.

Everyone had their own kids.

Everyone had their own careers.

And it seemed like everyone had their own fill of friends already.

I kept putting myself out there though. I knew enough to know I wasn't going to make friends by sitting on my couch, nursing my baby, eating cookie dough ice cream and watching television. This wasn't like the movie, Field of Dreams...If you build it, they will come. So, I went to church, I joined the YMCA, I went out to coffee, I had playdates, went out on double dates, joined and led small groups ... and still ... I felt so alone.

So, what was wrong? What was missing? Why, with all my efforts and stellar personality was I not attracting the kind of friendships I was craving?

And this was before the age of social media! I mean, not to brag, but we did have Myspace. It was all the rave. Back in the old days Facebook was just on the rise and all it was, at that time, was a bunch of people poking each other, and it felt weird to me. Trust me...poking each other was a thing. And if it makes you uncomfortable reading that, imagine receiving a "poke" from someone you used to know, or some older gentlemen you go to church with. Yeah...it's bizarre. But I digress...although that was a fun digression.

Before social media was all up in my business, the loneliness I felt as a new mom was overwhelming. Now it can be debilitating. The effects it has can cause us to stop trying at all. It has a voice that speaks to the depths of our soul that says:

You aren't cute enough.

You aren't fun enough.

You aren't interesting enough.

You aren't organized enough.

You aren't fashionable enough.

You aren't creative enough.

You are too boring, too young, too old, just too much for people to handle.

Ultimately there is a stigma around loneliness, and it is saying, **"You are not worthy of being loved."**

Have you heard any of those statements in your head? I know I have. Where do these feelings of "not enough" come from and how do we deal with them? I am going to show you three ways you can confront your loneliness head on and silence the voices speaking to you about your worth and value. But be warned, this isn't easy. For most of us, we are confronting deep seeded truths we have believed about ourselves. And for many of us, we are going to have to make some drastic changes and take some extreme ownership if we want to break out of this cycle.

But I think you have what it takes to do this, and good news…we don't have to do it alone. The Holy Spirit is here to help us, guide us, counsel us, empower us, grace us, and transform us. Let's jump in.

## What I Know Now:

I was watching an interview with former Surgeon General, Vivek Murthy, as he shared the dangers of social isolation. I don't know what his beliefs are in regard to Christ, but I do know that whatever they are, he was speaking some truth bombs about the state of our nation. Murthy said, "Loneliness has been increasing as the means to socially connect has been increasing." He continued to explain how loneliness has become an epidemic today that has been proven to shorten our life span in the same way smoking and obesity will! How crazy is that?

We were created for connection. We were created for a clan, a tribe, a crew. Even in the days of old, you survived longer if you were in a tribe. Tribes equaled having a stable food supply because there were more hunters and farmers, and it meant more protection from predators at night because there were more watchmen and warriors. But today, we call our tribe a group of people we've never met face to face, only seen on a four-inch screen we hold 12 inches from our face. And we wonder why the deep longings of our souls for connection aren't satisfied?

You would think, "I feel lonely" would equal the thought and action, "I am going to pick up the phone and call a friend." But more often than not, the response to our loneliness is further isolation. "I feel lonely" often leads us down a spiral of believing lie after lie until we are hosting a self-pity and self-loathing party of one!

The majority of people only show us their highlight reel. I know most of you know that, but I didn't quite catch onto that reality early on. Maybe I'm not the sharpest tool in the shed, but it took me some time to figure out I wasn't the only one struggling with feeling alone. I wasn't the only one craving a deep connection. My assumptions of others were simply that…an assumption. And others perceived my highlight reel as something it was not either. And I'm not suggesting we put all of our dirty laundry out there for all to see. I believe in being authentic to all and transparent to few, but the problem is, most of us aren't transparent to anyone, so we suffer in silence, in our own heads. The enemy *loves* when we have isolated ourselves in our thinking.

Speaking of the enemy, you know we have one, right? His name is Satan, the Devil, Lucifer, etc. One of the biggest names he goes by, that is a bit underrated in my opinion, is Accuser of the Brethren. In any war, one of the most effective strategies is to isolate your opponent and cut off communication. If they aren't receiving orders from higher up and aren't able to know what is going on in the grand scheme of things, the opponent often becomes paralyzed, or a sitting duck. And the enemy of our soul is no different.

I wish other moms would have told me what lies would be *so* easy for me to believe, that ultimately aided in my cycle of loneliness.

**Lie #1 - I don't want to be a burden to others.**

It sounds noble, right? Self-sacrificing even. I think there is something in all of us that tends to believe we are *too much* for people. And yet, when friends reach out to me who are hurting, lonely, and in need of help, my first thought isn't, "I don't have time for you!" Instead, a rush of compassion floods into my heart and a gratefulness they let me into the secret and sacred place of their life. But all too often, when the shoe is on the other foot, I tend to welcome this lie of being "too much" for people.

**Lie #2 - No one will understand me.**

I'm a stay-at-home mom. They can't understand my struggle.

I'm a working mom. She wouldn't get me.

I'm a mom of a special-needs child. Those other moms for sure can't understand.

I'm a single mom. No one feels the strain like me.

I'm a _____. (You fill in the blank.)

The bottom line is we have ALL had these thoughts. And you know what? All of us are 100% right and 100% wrong all at the same time. No one can understand exactly what you are walking through. This is your story, your journey, and your life. But that doesn't mean others can't have understanding of where you are at. Sympathy says, "I feel for you. I am sorry you are in this predicament." But empathy is someone who gets down in the pit with you and says, "I know what this pit feels like. I've been in my own pit before. Can I sit here with you for a bit?" Empathy may not have the exact details of your life replicated, but it can understand and relate to how you feel.

## Lie #3 – Letting people in is just too risky.

If there was ever a lie that kept me bound in isolation, it was this one. Have you been hurt by a friend? Me too. Have you been betrayed? Me too. Have you trusted your sister-friend with the depths of your soul only to have them walk away? Me too.

And you know what, it sucks. This kind of pain cuts deep. And we can even forgive the person and still have this residue remain; this thought that creeps up on the inside and says, "If you open up your heart like that again, you will get hurt." If you are anything like me, I had this continual internal posture of one hand beckoning people to come close to my heart while the other hand stiff armed them and said, "You aren't allowed to come any further."

God said in the beginning of creation, it is *not good* for man to be alone. (Genesis 2:18) Well, the serpent heard that and has been working hard ever since to get us back to seclusion. Our enemy knows the strength that comes when we are together. Look at these scriptures and how powerful they are!

*For where two or three are **gathered together** in My name, **I am there** in the midst of them.*
*Matthew 18:20 (NKJV)*

*Two are better than one, because **they have a good reward for their toil**. For if they fall, **one will lift up his fellow**. But woe to him who is alone when he fall and has not another to lift him up! Again, if two lie together, **they keep warm**, but how can one keep warm alone? And though a man might prevail against one who is alone, two will withstand him — **a threefold cord is not quickly broken**.*
*Ecclesiastes 4:9-12 (ESV)*

*As iron sharpens iron, so a man **<u>sharpens the</u>***
*<u>countenance of his friend</u>.*
*Proverbs 287:17 (NKJV)*

*Therefore, confess your sins to one another*
*and pray for one another,*
***<u>that you may be healed</u>.***
*The prayer of a righteous person has*
*great power as it is working.*
*James 5:16 (ESV)*

Don't think for one second the enemy isn't aware of the power of two or three. He is. And don't think for one second that your loneliness isn't a direct strategy to keep you from being everything God called and created you to be and accomplish on this earth. I wish other moms would have told me that if Satan can isolate me, then he can defeat me, lie to me, weaken me, deceive me, and make me good for nothing.

## Walking It Out:

Now that we know his strategy, let's talk about three ways we can defeat the loneliness cycle and engage in meaningful fellowship with a friend.

## 1. Get back on the saddle.

You and I both know this kind of friend we are longing for isn't going to magically appear at our door. This kind of friendship takes time to develop and work. So, girl, get yourself out there! You've got to start shallow before you go deep. If you pass on every ladies night out, if you never attend a women's Bible study, if you are always too tired and too busy for that coffee date, and if you are always waiting for someone to make the first move, then you really aren't wanting to change. You really aren't wanting to make friends.

Hey, I'm not doing you any favors by stroking your ego and saying this is going to be easy. For most of us (especially those of us who are more introverted), this is going to require us to set time aside to invest in relationships beyond our toddlers and husband! This means we are going to be inconvenienced. This means we are going to be in uncomfortable settings at times to discover who we have a connection with.

I cannot tell you how many friend dates I have been on. Too many to count. I am actively putting myself out there, surrounding myself with other women who I think might have potential to be in my inner circle. Proverbs says, if you want to have friends, you must be friendly! (Proverbs 18:24a)

Is it gonna be scary? Yes!

Will it be uncomfortable? Yes!

Will you get hurt again? Maybe!

Is it worth it? Absolutely!

This kind of friendship, *the friend who sticks closer than a brother (or sister),* is worth the risk of being hurt again. (Proverbs 18:24b) Love again, go deep again, trust again, and get back on the saddle again.

**2. Find the right people.**

Get back on the saddle, yes! But don't get on just any saddle!

Have you ever heard of the term, "You are thirsty?" Well if you haven't, let me break it down for you. It means you are so desperate for affection, attention, or approval it creeps people out. Being thirsty will repel the right people and attract the wrong ones.

I would be doing you a great disservice if I didn't address the elephant in the room. No one can fill the void in your heart but Jesus. If you don't get this right first, you can be surrounded by the best of people every moment of every day and still feel empty and alone. In fact, it would be wise of us to look at our loneliness and dissect it a bit to see where it is coming from. If we aren't spending time with the Lover of our soul, our Heavenly Father, the Great Comforter, and getting our needs met there first, we are looking for a false substitute in others they simply cannot fill.

And you must evaluate WHY you are lonely. Is it because you are too busy chasing success you don't have time to relate to others? Is it because you are walking in known sin and the guilt has caused you to feel separated from God and others? Is it because you are lousy at conflict resolution and have ostracized and pushed people away with your harshness and pride? If your loneliness is due to any of those issues I listed, then friends, you have some internal work to do. If you don't first deal with some of these root issues, you will continue this vicious cycle of loneliness because you are not taking responsibility for the part you play in why you are isolated.

First deal with your sin, your busyness, and your pride. Get wise counsel involved if this is a mountain you have continually found yourself circling. Become the kind of friend you want and need. Get healthy emotionally, spiritually, and mentally so you just don't have good friends, but in turn, can be a good friend.

But let's say those aren't the reasons. If you are desperate, you will attract desperate people, and that isn't always good. How do you attract the right kind of people? I am so glad you asked.

Look for women who are like-minded.

Who will help you find your answers.

Who will take you by the hand and walk you to Jesus.

This is how you create a solid sisterhood support system in your life. And you want to form these friendships now before crisis comes, because friend, crisis always comes. I wish it wasn't so, but life does not afford us the promise of a pain-free existence. We live in a fallen world, filled with broken and hurting people. And hurt people, hurt people. So, pain is going to come. Shaking is around the corner. Storms are headed our way. We cannot stop those things from entering our world, but we *can* control who is in the storms with us.

Get to that small group at church you have been giving every excuse in the book to miss. That woman at church who intrigues you? Ask her out for a coffee date! Start this week, even today! And don't let age stop you. She may be older or younger than you. She may be in a different phase of life than you. Guess what? That is okay! The most important framework for your blossoming friendship is; are you both going in the same direction with your relationship with Christ?

Can you have friendships with unbelievers? Of course, you can. But who you yolk up with is an entirely different story!

*Do not be unequally yoked together with unbelievers.*
*For what fellowship has righteousness with lawlessness?*
*And what communion has light with darkness?*
*2 Corinthians 6:14 (NKJV)*

Who you link shields with matters. You better make sure you are fighting the same battle and on the same team. Because when we surround ourselves with the right people, God will use their voice to speak to you. He will encourage you through them. He will lift you up out of that lonely pit through them. And He will meet your needs through them.

### 3. Get honest.

How can I pray for your marriage if you are always acting like it is perfect? How can I support you through your miscarriage if you never told me you were pregnant in the first place? How can I celebrate the wins you are having with your son's behavior at school if I never knew he was having behavioral issues to begin with?

I've said it before, and I will say it again. Not everyone needs to know what goes on behind the curtain of your life, but someone does! A few good friends need to know you are crying yourself to sleep every night. A few good friends need to know you are experiencing panic attacks and you aren't sure why. A few good friends need to know you are suffering with postpartum depression and have thoughts about hurting your child. By the way, those examples aren't hypotheticals, I experienced every single one of those and felt so much shame in them.

I've heard it said, "Shame, like mold, grows in the dark."

The answer? Bring it ALL out into the light. One of the most powerful scriptures I have every read is found in 1 John 1:7 (NASB). It says,

> *"But if we walk in the Light as He Himself is in the Light, __we have fellowship with one another__, and the blood of Jesus His Son cleanses us from all sin."*

Whatever area we keep hidden in the darkness gives access for the enemy to control and manipulate us. His aim is to keep us surrounded in the dark. Therefore, he comes as the Accuser of the Brethren whispering words to you about what will happen if people know the "real you." What will they think of you? He is banking on your fear of rejection to keep you from exposing your struggle.

In Mark 3 there is this man who enters the synagogue and has a deformed hand. Jesus invites this man to come and stand in front of everyone and says to him, "Hold out your hand." And the Bible says, when the man did this, his hand was restored. I bet this man walked around with this deformed hand hidden in his pocket his entire life. Ashamed of his weakness, he kept his struggle concealed. Jesus understood this man needed to expose the broken part of him he had been hiding in order to get healed. And Jesus knows the same process applies to you and me.

Loneliness is a killer, but it doesn't have to be. Don't let fear, shame, insecurity, sin, and anything else hold you back from entering into these rich relationships. When we are truly KNOWN and truly SEEN, with all the good, bad and the ugly, and loved and accepted by our friends despite all that, there is such freedom! Don't underestimate the power of friendships and togetherness, because our enemy certainly isn't. He is working overtime to make sure you stay trapped in your cell of loneliness. My friend, you hold the key to your prison cell. Set yourself free!

## Questions for Reflection:

1.  What are the biggest lies you have believed about why you are lonely?

    _____

    _____

    _____

    _____

2.  Are there areas in your life that are contributing to your loneliness that needs addressing? If so, what are they?

    _____

    _____

    _____

    _____

3.  Are you in daily fellowship with Jesus? Are you getting filled up with His presence, love, and words of truth first? If not, what is one action plan you can do tomorrow to set some time aside to get close to the heart of God?

    _____

    _____

    _____

    _____

4. Who do you need to reach out to this week and plan a friend date with?

_____

_____

_____

_____

5. Have you been holding up a persona that you have it all together? Who can you be honest with this week and let them see the struggle of your heart? Who can you expose your "deformed hand" to?

_____

_____

_____

_____

## Closing Prayer:

*Father, You see my lonely heart. I acknowledge I am sad, lonely, and have isolated myself to a degree and I need Your help. I need You to first come and flood up my heart. I need You to replenish the empty places within so I don't look to others to fill my void You only are meant to fill. Forgive me for neglecting my time with You. And thank You that Your arms are always wide open, welcoming me back into an intimate relationship with You. And Jesus, I am asking for a few great friends. Would You help me to have boldness to put myself out there? Would You heal the broken and tender places inside of me where others have hurt me? And would You lead me to friends who will point me to You always, the kind of friends who will call greatness out of me? Thank You for hearing my cry. Thank You for loving me completely, just as I am. I love You. Amen.*

OTHER MOMS NEVER TOLD ME I WOULD HAVE TO REPEAT, "DON'T LICK YOUR SISTER" DAY AFTER DAY.

MOMMENTOR.ORG

## Chapter 2

# Other Moms Never Told Me ...
# About Mom Anger

*By Diane Hwang*

*"God's law was given so that all people could see
how sinful they were. But as people sinned more
and more, God's wonderful grace became more abundant."*
*Romans 5:20*

### I Didn't See That Coming:

Before having children, anger wasn't an emotion I really struggled with. To be honest, I'd often breeze right through passages of scripture on anger because I naively assumed it just wasn't an area where I needed much help. Don't get me wrong, I had obviously been angry before, but overall, I considered myself a pretty calm, patient and happy person.

But that all changed once I had children of my own and my sweet, content babies turned into demanding toddlers with growing needs and challenging behavior. I never would have pictured myself as an angry mom, but here I was growing extremely short-tempered on a daily basis when my son pushed his sister down *once again* or my daughter continually yelled, "Mommy! Mommy! Mommy!" while pulling on my shirt for what felt like the hundredth time that day.

I can clearly remember the day when I first realized I was one of those 'angry moms' I swore I'd never become instead of the patient and calm mom I pictured myself to be. It had been a long, rough day of parenting and from the moment I woke up, everything seemed to trigger my anger and frustration. Whether it was having to repeat myself ten times, or having to clean up yet another spilled condiment cup of ketchup, I yelled more than I'd like to admit and spoke harsh words I instantly regretted.

As the day winded down and we were waiting for my husband to get home from work, my two toddlers played peacefully on the floor while I lay on my son's bed and replayed all of my angry moments from the day over and over in my head. It wasn't long before tears began streaming uncontrollably down my face as the shame and regret overwhelmed me with thoughts like:

"Your children will grow up resenting you."

"You'll never be able to control your anger."

"Your children will grow up with anger problems."

"Your children would be better off with another mom."

"You were never meant to be a mom."

"Who do you think you are writing articles for moms and leading moms' groups when you can't even be calm and patient with your own children?"

As much as I knew those whispers of shame were not from God, I couldn't help but feel like I'd never be the mom I wanted to be, and even worse, I'd never be the mom God created me to be.

Thankfully, my husband came home that evening and patiently listened to me as I leaned up against our kitchen counter crying and confessing all of my failed moments from the day. As he wrapped me in his arms and prayed over me, I realized, although all of those whispers of shame were lies from the pit of hell, I *did* have a problem with anger that needed to be addressed. I knew if I wanted to grow and become the woman and mother God created me to be, I'd need to face my sin head on and lean into the Holy Spirit for help in the process. But I still couldn't help but feel like I was alone and isolated on this journey.

Months later, I was catching up with a friend over FaceTime and she started opening up and sharing how much she was struggling with controlling her anger towards her children. She sounded discouraged as she talked about her constant battle to control her emotions and refrain from yelling, and I couldn't help but let out a big sigh of relief as I realized I was not alone. Her vulnerability led to a beautiful moment, as I was able to reply back with a heartfelt, "me too," and we both realized we were in the thick of it together.

After that conversation and the realization I wasn't the only mom struggling with anger, I finally found the courage to share my struggles with other women in my life. I was surprised to find many other moms were also suffering in silence and allowing their struggle with anger to wrongly define who they are as mothers. It also became clear through those conversations that anger was never an isolated emotion for any of us. Shame always rushed in after the anger had settled to leave all of us feeling alone, discouraged and afraid of what other people might think if they really knew how much we were struggling.

I'm not sure if you can relate to anything I shared above, but I'd love to walk you through three truths to remember when we experience anger in motherhood: We must know our help is found in Jesus Christ, there is power in confession and prayer; When we blow it, God can always turn it around for good.

## What I Know Now:

### 1. Our help is found in Jesus Christ.

I don't think there's anyone out there who enjoys being an angry mom. This is what I've found to be the most difficult part of the struggle – I wanted so badly to be calm and patient, but it seemed no matter how hard I tried to change my behavior and my reactions, they continued to resurface. I'd have a good couple days of being calm and collected, even through the meltdowns and defiant behavior, but sure enough, my anger would once again rear its ugly head and I was left feeling defeated by this tension between how I wanted to respond and how I was actually responding.

As I kept trying to work harder and harder to change my reactions, the Holy Spirit reminded me of a passage of scripture out of Romans where Paul talks about the Law and sin:

*"For I do not understand my own actions. For I do not do what I want, but I do the very thing I hate. Now if I do what I do not want, I agree with the law, that it is good. So now it is no longer I who do it, but sin that dwells within me. For I know that nothing good dwells in me, that is, in my flesh. For I have the desire to do what is right, but not the ability to carry it out. For I do not do the good I want, but the evil I do not want is what I keep on doing ...Wretched man that I am!* **Who will deliver me from this body of death? Thanks be to God through Jesus Christ our Lord!** *So then, I myself serve the law of God with my mind, but with my flesh I serve the law of sin."*
Romans 7:15-19, 24-25

Paul's words describing the battle between what I want to do and what I don't want to do, but actually do, made me realize this internal struggle I was experiencing is something we all struggle with as a result of our sinful nature. That's when my perspective began to shift and I realized my 'anger problem' was actually a 'sin problem' and I already have my help and answer through the person of Jesus Christ.

Another translation of this same passage says:

*"I've tried everything and nothing helps. I'm at the end of my rope. Is there no one who can do anything for me? Isn't that the real question?* **The answer, thank God, is that Jesus Christ can and does. He acted to set things right in this life of contradictions where I want to serve God with all my heart and mind, but am pulled by the influence of sin to do something totally different."**
*Romans 7:24-25 MSG*

Isn't that good news?! When we've tried everything and nothing seems to be helping, our inability and shortcomings point us to Jesus – He is our answer and He set things right for us so we can move forward from our sinful tendencies and become the moms He created us to be. Instead of feeling helpless with no way to control our emotions or words, we can look to the One who is constant and steady and allow Him to transform us to be more like Him.

## 2. There is power in confession and prayer.

When we yell at our children, slam the doors, or speak harsh words, shame wants us to believe the lie that if people found out about our struggle with anger, they would judge us and we would never experience the love and belonging we desire. We fear if they *really* knew about our sin, we would never be welcomed back to that local mom's group, would never truly belong in our church community, or would never have any other mom friends to do life with. So, we hide our struggles from everyone, including God.

The shame that comes with anger is often worse than the anger itself because it convinces us that working hard to hide our struggles from everyone around us, and overcoming them on our own, is our only option to finally be free from the grip of anger. But it's actually the very act of stepping out and confessing our struggles to God and to our trusted friends and family that will actually get us unstuck from the seemingly never-ending cycle of anger and shame.

As I think about the importance of confessing our sins to God, I think of the following two scriptures:

*"Those who look to Him for help will be radiant with joy; no shadow of shame will darken their faces."*

*Psalm 34:5*

*"People who conceal their sins will not prosper, but if they confess and turn from them, they will receive mercy."*

*Proverbs 28:13*

The Bible also talks about not just confessing our sins to God, but also speaks to this act of confessing our sins and struggles to one another:

*"Confess your sins to each other and pray for each other so that you may be healed. The earnest prayer of a righteous person has great power and produces wonderful results."*

*James 5:16*

While it often feels easier to keep your sin and struggles to yourself, while working hard to overcome them, scripture tells us when we bring our sins into the light and confess them to God and to others, we actually experience forgiveness, healing and freedom. As we open up about our struggles, the lie we once believed, that we are the only ones who lose our temper or yell at our kids, is overcome by the truth that we aren't alone and other moms struggle just like us.

### 3. When we blow it, God can use it for good.

As much as I wish we could learn to perfectly control our anger overnight, it's a process. There will be times when we lose our temper and blow it, despite our best efforts to do better. While this might initially seem discouraging, I've actually learned in the midst of our imperfections and failure, we have such a special opportunity to teach our children about repentance, forgiveness and ultimately point them to Jesus.

We read about the importance of asking others for forgiveness and reconciling our relationships in the book of Matthew:

*"So if you are offering your gift at the altar and there remember that your brother has something against you, leave your gift there before the altar and go.*

*First be reconciled to your brother, and then come and offer your gift."*

*Matthew 5:23-24*

This passage of scriptures speaks to the importance of not just being reconciled to others, but seeking forgiveness and making peace in our relationships right away, without delay. I've seen time and time again, when I choose to do what is commanded in this scripture, after I lose my temper with my kids, God so faithfully turns the situation around and my relationship with my children is filled with fresh grace, fresh peace, and fresh joy.

Not only is it an act of obedience on our part to seek forgiveness and reconcile our relationship with our children, but when we do this consistently, we are modeling to our children how to:

(1) Turn to God to repent and receive His forgiveness.

(2) Turn to the person we've wronged in humility and ask for their forgiveness.

The truth is, we will never be perfect parents, and our days ahead are sure to be full of moments when we fall short and mess up. But when we can freely receive forgiveness from God, and model humility to our children by owning our sin and asking for their forgiveness, we teach them lessons that will shape how they relate to others and resolve conflict; and every time I make the conscious decision to do this, I make space for God to bring good out of my failure.

## Walking It Out:

### 1. Identify your triggers.

While our anger often seems to erupt out of nowhere, there have most likely been different things contributing to it and building below the surface that lead to you 'losing it'. When we identify our triggers, we become aware of the circumstances or behaviors that push our emotions over the edge, and we can control our anger before it controls us. It's also important to note that triggers look different for every person, and can also look different in various seasons of life.

So learning to control our emotions requires us to constantly look inward to evaluate why we feel what we feel.

Some examples of triggers for different people:

- When your children don't listen

- When you don't get enough sleep

- When your children are whining

- When you are under financial stress

- When your children are fighting with one another

- When you are overwhelmed with too much on your plate at work

- When you are running late

- When there is too much noise

- When the house is messy

If you can't quite figure out what your triggers are, try keeping track of your angry moments on a piece of paper and ask the Holy Spirit to reveal any ongoing patterns, just as David did in Psalm 139:

*"Search me, O God, and know my heart; test me*
*and know my anxious thoughts. Point out anything*
*in me that offends you, and lead me along*
*the path of everlasting life."*
*Psalm 139:23-24*

When you pray this prayer and ask the Holy Spirit to reveal what is causing your anger, He will faithfully reveal to you what is going on beneath the surface so you can move forward with greater understanding and awareness.

## 2. Identify the best way to handle your emotions.

Once we discover what is triggering and contributing to our anger, we can determine the best way to move beyond awareness and actually change our behavior and manage our emotions better. While it's not realistic to expect our anger to just go away, there are many things we can do to, not only control our triggers, but to calm our emotions in the heat of the moment.

As I was thinking about the different things that trigger my anger in this season of life with two toddlers, lack of sleep is one that almost always leads to me having a shorter fuse. If I am not getting enough sleep, the most insignificant things can frustrate me and I find myself failing to manage my emotions all day. Since sleep is something I can control, it is important for me to go to bed early on a regular basis and make sure I'm getting the sleep I need.

While there are things I can control, like how much sleep I get, there are also many triggers outside of my control. For example, I can't always control the behavior of my children, but there are things I can do to help settle my emotions in the heat of the moment. One trigger for me is when one of my toddlers is having a massive tantrum and nothing seems to be calming their big emotions. When this happens, I've learned that stepping away to take 10 deep breaths helps me to remain calm so I can tend to their needs without having a meltdown myself.

In those moments when you feel your anger rising and you are about to erupt, there are several things you can try to regain control of your emotions:

- **Take a timeout:** Take a moment to sit by yourself until your emotions begin to settle if possible.

- **Sing the ABCs:** Pause what you are doing and sing the ABC's when you feel the anger building. Usually by the time you are done, your emotions are settled and you can respond more calmly.

- **Take a walk:** If your spouse or a family member is home, stepping outside for some fresh air and a bit of movement can work wonders when you need to calm down and press reset on your emotions.

- **Take a deep breath:** Often when people are angry, their breathing becomes quick and shallow. So, focus on taking slow, deep breaths, inhaling through your nose and exhaling through your mouth for several cycles to help regain control of your emotions.

Not all of these ideas will work for everyone, so sometimes it might take trying a few different things to see what works best for you. But the more you practice staying calm, the easier it becomes.

## 3. Don't be afraid to seek professional help.

Reaching out to our friends and family is beneficial, but ultimately, if our anger is overwhelming or getting worse, seeking professional help is a courageous step that can provide the extra support we need. Many of us are walking through life with grief, wounds from current or past abuse, postpartum depression, and many other complex triggers, and one of the best things we can do for ourselves and our families is lean into the help and support of counseling or support groups.

When I was in my twenties, my second engagement was broken off and I found myself in a huge mess of sin and emotional hurts. After trying my best to overcome it on my own, I finally realized I needed some professional support to help me. A pastor from my church recommended a Christian counselor from our community and I finally started the much needed process of facing the trauma and wounds from my past with the support of someone who pointed me to Jesus and the truth found in His Word.

I always thought counseling was a last resort for when things got really bad, but I realized counseling is such a great preventative resource to support us as we learn how to process our emotions, relate to others better, and deal with issues before they grow out of control. Christian counseling or support groups are great tools in our tool belt to, not only help us navigate our way through tough seasons, but to ultimately help us grow and mature to be all God created us to be.

## Questions for Reflection:

1. In what ways have you attempted to overcome your anger in your own strength?

   _____

   _____

   _____

   _____

2. What situations or circumstances tend to trigger your anger?

   _____

   _____

   _____

   _____

3. What have you learned about the act of confessing your sins?

   _____

   _____

   _____

   _____

4. What are some scriptures you can meditate on when you get frustrated?

_____

_____

_____

_____


5. If you don't have a support system, who can you call this week to confide in and ask for help?

_____

_____

_____

_____

## Closing Prayer:

*Father, I thank You that I can come freely and boldly to You for help, and when I do, You remind me of who I am and the truth that You chose me to be my childrens' mother. I thank You that my sin and anger do not disqualify me from being a mother, but they are proof that I need You as my perfect Heavenly Father to help me be who You created me to be. I ask You to continue to reveal any unknown triggers and help me to be more aware of my emotions and how they impact my behavior. I pray Your Holy Spirit would fill me and give me everything I need to raise my children with patience, love and tenderness. Thank You for being my safe place, thank You for forgiving me of my sin, and for empowering me to change and mature to become more like You. I ask these things in the Name of Jesus Christ. Amen.*

OTHER MOMS NEVER TOLD ME I'LL NEVER GET TO SLEEP IN ON THE WEEKENDS EVER AGAIN!

# Chapter 3

# Other Moms Never Told Me ...
# How Motherhood Opens Old Wounds

*By Lisa Hamel*

*"But as for me, the nearness of God is my good; I have made*
*the Lord GOD my refuge, That I may tell of all Your works."*
*Psalm 73:28*

## I Didn't See That Coming:

Just seconds after my son was born, his eyes collided with
mine. I knew he couldn't really see me, but he looked so
desperate. Like he was searching for an anchor in his new,
scary world. "Help me!" his eyes seemed to say.

Imagine leaving everything that seemed comfortable and
entering a new world where your eyes can't process the
information coming into them. Your ears can't make sense of
the noises. You don't have a language. You can't regulate your
temperature. Each and every one of us enters the world this
way and when my son looked up at me in complete

overwhelm, it triggered something in **me** that seemed almost infantile in nature. I was completely overwhelmed too.

I've had a long and arduous relationship with anxiety so the expectation of bestowing safety and comfort for a helpless baby was like the blind leading the blind. Sure, I could feed him and change his diapers, but to model calm for him, I knew that I would be faking it!

Just the thought of trying to keep him alive while taking all the prescribed medications (as a sleep-deprived, hormonal hot mess) was enough to shoot my anxiety through the roof.

*Feed him every two to three hours or more. Take ibuprofen every three hours. Take this medication every six hours. Change his diapers. Manage your own body in its postpartum state.*

And the list went on. That first night in the hospital was like the unpredictable lull found in a war zone between battles. Machines beeped erratically and doors slammed shut. My son made strange noises I was not accustomed to. I was radically exhausted, but the weight of his care kept my adrenaline pumping. I sensed this pivotal, beautiful, holy experience of bringing him into this world was part of a greater war, dormant, now awakened.

It wasn't that I hadn't prepared. I watched videos on how to care for your baby. I took classes. I had friends who were ahead of me in the journey. I was educated on the signs of postpartum depression. What I didn't expect was this overwhelming sense of responsibility that made it impossible to sleep even when my son was resting. I dreaded the nights, but each morning I was so excited to be with him. After four days and nights without sleep, I was ready to hit myself over the head with a skillet just to find the blessed relief of unconsciousness.

I finally realized I had postpartum anxiety. My nervous system was running hot all day and all night. The intensity of my child's needs simply revealed a gaping hole in my ability to meet my own need for a restful body, mind, and spirit. I could not give what I did not have. I'm so glad God never wastes a hurt. He used this intense season to magnify my weakness so that I would be motivated to seek out answers for my son (who we later discovered had autism), and for my own anxiety. Believe it or not, the answers were found in how babies and moms attach to each other.

I really can't blame other moms for my lack of preparation. Most people don't know or understand the recent discoveries about the brain and how we attach to others. Before I could help a neuro-atypical (autistic) brain, I needed to understand my own challenges and how our broken brains could intersect in a God-given dance of joy and rest that could grow us both. Because I believe God designed the brain, I knew the answers found in science would line up with what is in His Word.

Those piercing blue eyes searching for comfort propelled me in my search as they were unable to receive what I was imperfectly pouring out in nurture. Because of my son's neuro-atypical brain, he couldn't attach to me easily. I later learned babies with sensory processing disorder or neuro-atypical brains are often too overwhelmed to receive and attach. So, I had two problems, his challenges (which I didn't understand at the time) and my own anxiety. It all just felt off. Stilted. Awkward. What I was experiencing didn't align with what I observed in other moms. This amplified my recognition that I needed help, but it took me many years to find answers.

There was so much I didn't understand at the time. I didn't know a baby doesn't "exist" if Mom is not around. Their reality is based upon their attachment. Their identity is completely established by who they are connected to. Mom's existence brings order to their forming universe. The absence of this attachment inhibits the organization of the brain for the future. When a baby has their needs met, this bonds the mother and baby together and creates the joyful state which is the bedrock of all human development.

Other moms couldn't explain that without touch, his brain would produce cortisol, a stress hormone that kills brain cells. This can result in a baby adapting to a state of anxiety and adrenaline by twelve weeks of age. Other moms couldn't explain that simple eye contact with my baby would grow his brain. In fact, my research taught me that:

*"Nothing interests a baby more than looking at faces and eyes. Whenever he sees joyful eyes looking at him, the joy in him explodes... As they climb to higher and higher levels of joy, babies literally build brain capacity."[i]*

## What I Know Now:

From this, I discovered that even my own struggles with depression and anxiety were potentially rooted in this precious mother/child bond from my first few years of life. You see, we are unique in our biology (for example, some kids are more naturally relaxed than others). Despite this uniqueness, we all share certain commonalities. We were each born with a brain craving attachment. We were each born into a sinful, broken world to sinful, broken parents and because of this, our caregivers may not have given us what we needed. Thanks to neuroscience, we understand now more than ever how this crucial season of life shapes us in the first two years!

1. **All humans need a constant cycle of joy and rest.**

   Babies learn this cycle in the first two years of life. In fact, joy (delight, connection) is the only emotion a baby is motivated to search out on their own. One neuroscientist said that a baby's main job in those first two years is to experience that they are a delight. In Genesis, we see God called His creation "good." He rejoiced and delighted in his creation and then He rested. We are created in the image of our good Creator so it only makes sense that we would follow this same cycle of joy and rest. Moms, you are your child's first and most important source of joy. In those first months, you are their entire world.

2. **Babies having their needs met sets their trajectory for life!**

   Simply put, as babies' needs are met, their brains grow. Fancy terms like "dopamine" and "serotonin" weren't household words when I was a new mom. Other moms couldn't tell me my baby's brain was creating baselines for these vital neurochemicals through our cycle of joyful interactions and rest. Though the world makes us feel like our day-to day mundane "mother life" lacks deep meaning and purpose, the trajectory for your child's emotional resilience for life is formed in these seemingly meaningless moments.

Each diaper changed. Each cry answered. Each bonded moment through feeding. (No matter the method!) Each shared smile. In these, our babies learn they are a delight and that their needs matter. From here, they can grow into children who can do hard things and learn how they can contribute in a unique way to their world. In these first few years, our job of joyfully delighting in our children and meeting their needs is preparing them to have a greater emotional capacity as adults. We've heard that we need to prepare, not just protect our children. As we delight in our babies, we are preparing their brains to grow the capacity to deal with life's hardships.

3. **The clincher for me was understanding that this earthly example is an echo of our greater spiritual reality.**

We can see that God created the human brain in-line with his eternal plan. Babies can give nothing to us. They simply receive. They recognize they are a delight. They share joy and they grow. We had nothing to give God. Consider the following verses in light of this concept.

*"But God shows His love for us in that while*
*we were still sinners, Christ died for us."*
*Romans 5:8*

You see, God made us to attach. If our babies don't get their needs met, the world is an unsafe place for them. This activates anxiety and anger in the brain instead of peace and joy. Our Heavenly Father was so attached to us, He made a way for our greatest need (salvation!) to be met through sacrificing His precious son.

*"We love because He first loved us."*
*1 John 4:19*

We love because He first loved us. Love is attachment. We attach to our Heavenly Father because He first attached to us. You can't help but love someone who delights to be with you.

*"For by grace you have been saved through faith.*
*And this is not your own doing; it is the gift of God,*
*not a result of works, so that no one may boast.*
*For we are his workmanship, created in Christ Jesus*

*for good works, which God prepared beforehand,*
*that we should walk in them."*
*Ephesians 2:8-10*

The term "grace" has often been defined as unmerited favor. This means you are really significant and precious to someone without having to work for it. That's what our babies are to us and that is what we are to God.

Do you know deep down in the core of your soul that you are a delight to God? The more we learn to receive this, the stronger our attachment to our Father. The stronger our joy.

*"The Lord your God is in your midst, a mighty one*
*who will save; he will rejoice over you with*
*gladness,*
*he will quiet you by his love; he will exult*
*over you with singing."*
*Zephaniah 3:17*

## Walking It Out:

### 1. Motherhood matters.

What you do in those days and months and years of motherhood matter! Those seemingly endless seasons, giving of your body, your sleep, your heart...they matter!

You are setting up your child's brain for life.

Even the propensity for addiction develops largely out of the first two years of life.

Your child's view of God will first and foremost develop from how they have attached to you!

You are raising eternal beings. As you meet their physical needs for food, rest, warmth, etc., and you meet their emotional needs of joy, rest, and validation, you are sewing into an eternal harvest.

### 2. Changing the code.

As adults, we are all walking around with a code written into our heads. We aren't consciously aware of it, but it is running twenty- four/seven. This code interprets how safe people are. How safe our world is. How much we are a delight or burden to others. If it's okay to stop and rest or if it's dangerous to do so. This code is "written" in our brains before we understand words or letters or numbers. It is written by the faces that lit up to see us as fragile, helpless babies.

Even if we were raised in less than ideal circumstances or have mothered our children with regrets up to this point, the amazing news is we can still grow! As my autistic son would say, "The code can still change!"

Parts of your brain retain fetal biochemistry. Simply put, this means what was started at the very beginning of life still exists in your body! It's never too late to grow. It's never too late to heal. It's never too late to change brain pathways. If you have a five-lane freeway to fear and anxiety and an overgrown switchback trail to joy and peace, it doesn't have to stay that way! I can testify that understanding these concepts even after my kids were older has changed all of us. We now understand the power of joy. That same joy that was imperfectly shared with us as infants can still be shared and grow our brains now. That same joy was what motivated Jesus to die for us. What a miracle!

### 3. Attachment love heals us.

We have *chesed* (Hebrew) or "sticky love" from God and brains that have neuroplasticity, which means they are pliable and can continue to grow and develop as long as we have breath. What hope we have!

Perhaps your own encounter with motherhood has left you feeling your own weakness to staggering levels. Perhaps you are overwhelmed by how motherhood has amplified what you have elegantly kept hidden just beneath the surface. Let Jehovah Rapha heal you. Let His perfect love drive out your fear.

As Hebrews 12:2 encourages, fix your eyes on Jesus. He's the author and perfecter of your faith. And for the joy of being in a relationship with you, He endured the cross! He endured the most unimaginable pain and abandonment so your sin wouldn't stand in the way of a relationship with Him. He is enamored by you. Just as you were enamored by your babies. All you have to do, dear friend, is accept. Accept from Jesus and others who can model for you calm and rest.

If your attachment to Jesus has been broken or difficult because of your broken world, know there is healing and grace. God used my own brokenness and that of my son to reveal His limitless patience and *chesed* love. You are in the grip of His grace. Just as you stared at your baby in wonder, Jesus delights in you – His precious child.

And someday, you will stand face to face with the Protector of your soul and the Author of your faith. You will look in His eyes and just like an infant with a mother, nothing else will matter but who He is. He will be your whole reality/world.

For all the ways I failed my son in those early years, I have seen God "restore what the locust has eaten." (Joel 2:25-26) We have grown in joy, rest and attachment to each other and Jesus. When his nervous system crashes into mine, we have tools and the established relationship to quiet and work through our problems. God is relational! He doesn't just leave us broken. Not only our resilience but our motivations are rooted in our bonds. Who we are attached to motivates us far more than our knowledge, so may you experience His sticky love, His unmitigated joy, His unending delight…and heal.

## Questions for Reflection:

1.  As best as you can assess, do you feel your needs were met as a child?

   _____

   _____

   _____

   _____

2.  Do you believe yourself to be a delight or a burden to others?

   _____

   _____

   _____

   _____

3.  In light of this chapter, how can you encourage other moms with the meaning of what they do?

   _____

   _____

   _____

   _____

4. How would you describe your attachment to Jesus? i.e. Safe? Insecure? Loving? Uncertain? Fearful?

_____

_____

_____

_____

5. Do you feel you and your family get enough joy? How about true rest? How can you improve in these areas?

_____

_____

_____

_____

## Closing Prayer:

*"Precious Father God, I praise You that I was fearfully and wonderfully and intentionally made. Thank You for allowing Your creation to reflect You in joy and rest. Thank You for delighting in me, when I had nothing to offer You. Thank You that You can make beauty from the ashes of my brokenness. Thank You that You are never overwhelmed by my needs but delight to meet them. Thank You for attaching to me. Thank You that Your sticky love won't give up on me. May I show this love to my children and my world. May I be bonded to You in love and not fear. Jesus, please show me where You want to bring healing and growth in my own life and in the lives of my children. In Jesus' name, Amen.*

# OTHER MOMS NEVER TOLD ME I WOULD NEVER BE ABLE TO SNEEZE AGAIN WITHOUT FEAR OF PEEING MY PANTS.

# Chapter 4

# Other Moms Never Told Me ...
## About Mom Guilt

---

*By Melissa Miller*

---

*"You will know the truth, and the truth will set you free."*
*John 8:32*

### I Didn't See That Coming:

At my kid's school, another mom spoke five stabbing words.

"You *forgot* crazy sock day?"

She pointed to my son's white ankle socks as he ran into his classroom. Other kids ran past me with striped knee-high socks, socks with fringe, and socks representing their favorite sports team.

"Uh, oh, yeah. I guess I did. It was a mad-dash this morning."

My friend probably didn't mean anything by her comment, but those five words sounded an alarm in my soul: *I'm not doing enough. I'm not measuring up. Guilty, guilty, guilty.*

I slipped back to my car and nearly hyperventilated. The pressure crushed my shoulders and my spirit. The feeling of not doing enough, not measuring up, or just flat out not being enough, pulsed through my veins like venom. I went home that day feeling like my tail was tucked between my legs. *Why did her subtle comment hurt me so much?*

My son, especially when he was younger, was always convinced he was ready for things he wasn't ready for. He wanted to do what the big boys were doing. He was the type who would jump in the deep end before he knew how to swim. When it came to amusement parks, nothing made his blood boil more than being told he wasn't tall enough for a ride.

"41 inches. Too bad, you have to be 42 inches to ride this ride. Not quite tall enough, buddy. Maybe next year."

When my son heard those words, his face would turn strawberry red, his brows furrowed, and he protruded his bottom lip out like a saucer. He hated being told he was too short. One time, he wore hiking boots to Disneyland. Living in Southern California at the time, we hardly wore anything besides flip-flops. When I asked him why he wore hiking boots, he mumbled that it made him taller for the rides.

I can relate to my son's hatred towards that feeling: not quite enough. For many years, it seemed like no matter what I did to improve myself as a mom, at the end of the day I still felt like my son: disqualified.

*I'm sorry, Melissa, you're not tall enough to ride the motherhood train. So close. Try again next year. Step aside, and let someone more qualified handle this, will ya?!*

Of course, I had to keep mothering, despite my feelings of being unqualified. That invisible line remained. Even when I improved as a mom, it seemed like the line kept getting higher. I experienced tremendous guilt for not measuring up.

When I wasn't able to attend all the functions my kids got invited to, I felt guilty.

When I needed a break from my kids, I felt guilty.

When I took a day of rest, I felt guilty.

When I couldn't afford certain things for my kids, I felt guilty.

When I failed to keep up with all the school functions, I felt guilty.

When my kids didn't eat enough fruits, veggies, or all organic, I felt guilty.

Whenever I wasn't supermom (which was everyday) I felt guilty.

It seemed like I was always shy of reaching this elusive standard. If I could only reach the benchmark, I wouldn't feel guilty anymore, right? Maybe I needed to get me some hiking boots.

Crazy sock day was the day I knew I was fed up with this imaginary line. Who was the one drawing this line, anyway? Who sets this standard? Who is the one constantly telling me I'm not enough? I had some things to think about.

When I picked my son up from school that day, I apologized.

"No big deal, Mom." He said. "I don't like long socks anyways; they make me hot."

His reaction made me exhale. If I were honest with myself, I didn't think crazy sock day was that big of a deal either. In fact, if I were really honest, I loathed crazy sock day, tie-dye day, sports team day, and wear the brightest-neon-green-shirt-day (because none of us own that color and we all have to go to eight stores to find it). Nowadays we homeschool and its wear-whatever-the-heck-you-want day, every day. Praise the Lord.

I began asking other moms if they experienced this guilty feeling.

"Yeah, I get 'Mom Guilt' all the time," One mom responded.

*Mom Guilt.* It was the first time I'd heard that phrase, it brought me comfort because it meant I wasn't the only one experiencing it. During a recent podcast interview, Kate Middleton described Mom Guilt as a "constant challenge."[ii] In the new CALIA commercial, Carrie Underwood says, "I'm a mother, wife, singer, songwriter, but I'm also me, Carrie. To be the best in every role, I have to put myself first. I feel guilty when I do. I feel guilty when I don't. I have to tell myself, I can give myself permission."[iii]

Here are some of the things my friends felt 'Mom Guilt' about:

- Feeling guilty for not being able to give their undivided attention to their second or third child like they were able to with their first.

- Guilt for staying at home with their children and not working.

- The working moms expressed feeling guilty for not staying at home with their children.

- Guilt that they couldn't afford to pay for braces for their children, a car on their 16th birthday, or a private education.

- Guilty for spending too much time parenting their children and not enough time playing with them.

- Guilty when they went out with their friends, or out on a date with their husbands.

- Guilty not knowing how to handle their child's behavior.

- Guilty that they had trouble breastfeeding and needed to use formula.

- Guilty for not volunteering more at their kid's school.

- Guilty for not making meals from scratch.

- Guilty for not wanting to cuddle anymore, or for having a limit to how much touch they can handle for one day.

Can you relate to any of the guilty feelings these moms listed? I know I can. Where do these feelings of guilt come from, and what do we do with them? I'm going to give you three tools for your arsenal when you face Mom Guilt; Know who your enemy is, know *whose* you are, and know *who* you are. Let's dive in.

## What I Know Now:

1. **Know who your enemy is.**

When we feel convicted, this feeling is from the Holy Spirit. It is loving and the purpose is to reconcile us to God. We feel convicted when we sin, it's a signal from the Holy Spirit that something isn't in line with God's best for our lives. Guilt, shame, and condemnation are different. These feelings don't come from God and they don't serve a fruitful purpose.

Satan is referred to in scripture as the accuser of the brethren (Revelation 12:10). This word 'accuser' refers to a prosecutor or plaintiff in a lawsuit, or one who speaks in a derogatory way of another. While we see the names of God reflect God's character, (such as Jehovah Rapha, "The Lord that Heals" or Jehovah Shalom meaning "The Lord is Peace") Satan's character is shown in this verse in Revelation, he is "The Accuser," bringing accusations to believers.

Another reflection of the nature of Satan is that he is called the "father of all lies." Jesus speaks about this in John 8:44 when addressing the Jews who aimed to kill Him,

*"You belong to your father, the devil, and you want to carry out your father's desires. He was a murderer from the beginning, not holding to the truth, for there is no truth in him. When he lies, he speaks his native language, for he is a liar and the father of lies."*

Jesus gave us insight into our adversary, who is, quite literally, the master liar. Jesus also refers to him as a thief who aims to steal, kill, and destroy (John 10:10).

We now know three things about this devil dude:

1. He is an accuser. (Revelation 12:10)

2. He is a master liar. (John 8:44)

3. He is a thief who aims to steal, kill, and destroy. (John 10:10)

We don't need to live in fear about the devil, but we also don't need to ignore the reality of his existence. What does it look like to ignore the reality of the devil? We buy into the idea that if we simply tried harder, it would appease our guilt. Have you ever noticed that on the day you did everything perfectly, there still seems to be something to feel guilty about? Maybe you fed your kids all organic that day. Maybe that day you gave them your undivided attention, never lost your cool. Maybe that day you crossed everything off your list. It was your supermom day. Why then, at the end of the day is there still a nagging sense of guilt? As you scroll through Instagram and discover the mom who dresses all five of her children in matching, homemade clothes, the gavel pounds down hard. Guilty! *You did good that day, but not good enough. Time to buy a sewing machine, sweetie.*

The devil will use any means to convince you you don't measure up. You can jump as high as you possibly can, and you'll never be good enough for his impossible standards. This is the first step: know your real enemy. It turns out it's not the gal who called you out for forgetting crazy sock day or the mom on Instagram who sews bonnets for her babies.

## 2. Know whose you are.

The Jewish people spent countless years trying to measure up to the Law. Many viewed religion and behavior modification as their ticket to heaven. The Law provided a line, and when Jesus came, He shattered the line with His death, burial, and resurrection. Jesus made it clear: righteousness flows through relationship, not religion. Without Jesus, we find ourselves playing a game of high jump all over again. We just can't reach high enough, can't be holy enough, or good enough. No matter how hard we try, the 'Mom Guilt' creeps in, reminding us of another area of our not-enoughness. The miraculous work on the cross, all wrapped in love, gives us the gift of enough in Jesus. We could slave away our entire lives and never earn or deserve this gift of grace. When I declare, with confidence, the truth that I am enough, I do so with a disclaimer in my heart: *I am enough...because of Jesus*. I might not be enough for the supermoms in the neighborhood, or have enough money to join certain social clubs, or do enough volunteering at my kids' school to win any mom-of-the-year awards...those things don't matter. I'm enough to God because I'm a child of God. Jesus soared past the line of worthiness, so I don't have to.

The constant state of guilt comes from The Accuser, that's his job. He might continue to attempt to do his job, but that doesn't mean we should make it easy on him. Resting in our identity as children of God reminds us of whose voice we should trust. As the saying goes, "Don't believe everything you think."

We need to listen to The Advocate rather than The Accuser. John 14:26 tells us another name for the Holy Spirit: Advocate. An advocate intercedes on behalf of another. In a court setting, the advocate will assist or speak for an individual. It seems pretty simple when the options are laid out: we can listen to the voice that seeks to accuse us or the voice that advocates for us.

When the enemy raises the elusive bar once again, when he twists the truth like a lemon wedge and tells us we aren't good enough, we don't have to try to convince him or ourselves otherwise. We can agree, but add in the full truth ...

*It's true: I'm not enough. I don't measure up. I'm human and I'm imperfect. Jesus is enough, Jesus stands in my place, and Jesus soars past that line of worthiness. I'm God's child, completely loved by Him. Jesus chose me to be my child's mother, and therefore I am equipped and qualified by Him. I choose to listen to The Advocate's voice instead of The Accuser.*

3. **Know who you are.**

I spilled the beans. I shared with you how I hated crazy sock day and all the other crazy days at school, but it gets worse. I hated parent teacher conferences, bringing the cupcakes for all the birthday parties, attending the school assemblies, school pick-ups and drop-offs, trying to remember to bring in toilet paper rolls for one classroom, and a bag of feathers for the other. The list goes on. I can completely own it now without a twinge of shame, but I used to feel tremendously guilty over my feelings around the kids' school to-dos. *I'm a mom, this is what moms do, right? We are supposed to love these things because we love our kids, right? Why is it such a struggle for me to enjoy the things other moms seemed to have no problem with?*

When my friend started homeschooling, she sent me a link to the curriculum she chose. I felt drawn to the curriculum immediately. The structure of the curriculum broke through my barriers of intimidation around homeschooling. I prayed about it for a few months, wondering if it was a silly idea. Then I ran across this question in one of John Maxwell's books: "If you only had five years to live, how would you spend your time?" I immediately responded, "I would homeschool my kids." My response surprised me. I didn't know that desire was buried inside of me underneath a heaping mound of fearing failure.

That next school year, I took the leap. I decided to give homeschool my all, to refuse to be limited by fear, and to explore this curriculum I felt drawn to. I'm heading into my third year of homeschooling now. Looking back, it was one of the best decisions I ever made. As it turns out, there was a reason why I felt angst regarding traditional school stuff. God had something different for my family. Instead of responding to what I felt drawn to, I spent many years trying to push through, suck it up, and "be a good school mom."

The reason why I share this story is because sometimes the backpack of Mom Guilt stems from us not living authentic to who we really are. Maybe God can use those guilty feelings as an opportunity for us to examine our hearts, get rid of comparisons and find a more authentic path for us. Perhaps we are trying to fit into the mold of the way other moms do things, because it's what we *should* do. Maybe we ought to stop "should-ing" all over ourselves.

My friend confessed she felt guilty that she doesn't read books to her kids like I do. I asked her a few questions about what she does with her kids. It turns out she raps, makes music, dances, and sings with her kids. I admire her for this because I have zero musical ability. I reminded my friend that we need to make motherhood our own. We won't be good at everything, but we will be good at something. If we don't like baking with our kids...oh well. There are a million other ways to connect with our kids. Maybe you are more of a hiking or basketball kind of mom. Be authentic. Build memories around what you enjoy doing together, not based on what you "should" do because other moms are doing it.

Sometimes Mom Guilt is simply from the enemy and we need to remind ourselves *whose* we are. But sometimes Mom Guilt comes from comparisons, and we need to remember *who* we are. We need to get comfortable in our own skin, own our authentic identity and unique strengths, and stop comparing ourselves to other moms.

## Walking It Out:

### 1. Know the truth.

Jesus said if we know the truth, the truth will set us free (John 8:32). There is a difference between hearing about the truth and knowing it. It's not enough for the truth to breeze by us occasionally, we need to know it. We need the truth to translate from our heads to our hearts. The only way this can happen is if the truth becomes a central focus in our lives.

There are a lot of cheeky phrases out there on the internet, phrases that might make us feel good about ourselves momentarily. But they aren't to be confused with truth. Truth liberates. Spend time in The Word daily. Dwell on it. Meditate on it. Take the verses that need to move from your head to your heart and memorize them.

During one difficult season of my life, I wrote verses about my identity and stuck them all over my bedroom walls. I prayed circles around that room each day, praying each verse over myself. I wasn't taking those sticky notes down until I knew deep in my soul, they were all true. Get relentlessly stubborn about the renewing of your mind.

## 2. Pray for protection.

Now that we understand who the real enemy is, we can stand against him in prayer. You could pray to be better, jump higher, measure up more often … but if you don't allow God to fight this battle for you, you will be high jumping in vain. Ask God to protect you from the lies of the enemy, from the accusations he brings.

When a specific lie comes, identify it and speak the truth over it in prayer. Thank God that He equips you, qualifies you, and gives you everything you need to be the mom He's called you to be.

### 3. Remind yourself you're in process.

There are times we make mistakes. We lose our temper, we put our foot in our mouth, we allow our phone to monopolize our day. Whatever our mishap was, it's important not to let it bury us in guilt and shame. Failing doesn't mean we are a failure. Making mistakes doesn't mean God made a mistake when he chose us to be a mom.

Remind yourself you are in process. Apologize. A true, "Will you please forgive me?" apology goes a long way. Model for your kids what it means to be in process but to keep growing in humility and strength. Jesus doesn't expect you to be perfect. If you were perfect, you wouldn't need a Savior.

## Questions for Reflection:

1.  What areas do you experience Mom Guilt in?

    _____

    _____

    _____

    _____


2.  What did you learn about The Accuser and his tactics?

    _____

    _____

    _____

    _____


3.  What are some truths you can speak and pray over yourself?

    _____

    _____

    _____

    _____

4. What are your unique strengths as a mom?

_____

_____

_____

_____

5. What is one verse you'd like to memorize?

_____

_____

_____

_____

## Closing Prayer:

*Father, I thank You that You called me to be a mother. I thank You for the incredible gift of motherhood. I thank You that You wired me with unique strengths, and You called and equipped me to be a great mother. I pray for protection against any of the lies from The Accuser. I pray I would recognize the lies when they come and that You would help me to know the truth and the truth would set me free. I pray I would become completely comfortable with my authentic self. I pray I would set an example for my kids in humility, authenticity, and confidence in my identity in You. I pray for freedom from guilt, shame, and condemnation. Lead me to a new level of liberty. In Jesus name, Amen.*

OTHER MOMS
NEVER TOLD ME
I SHOULD INVEST
IN THE
BAND AID BRAND.

# Chapter 5

# Other Moms Never Told Me ...
# How to Find Meaning in the Mundane

*By Kyleen Baptiste*

> *"...For I have learned in whatever*
> *situation I am to be content."*
> *Philippians 4:11*

## I Didn't See That Coming:

Alright, I have a confession. I *have* heard other moms say it. I didn't become a mom until later in life, so it's fair to say I'd heard lots of motherhood sayings before they ever really applied to me. Before becoming a mom, I thought I understood what other moms were saying when they would comment, 'Soak it all up.' Yep, got it! Soak up all the exciting, adventurous moments! I watched so many amazing moms around me in their element, seemingly enjoying the whole gig of motherhood. I mistakenly believed I understood the depth of that phrase and the momming game in general. Hair cute, mascara in place, matching outfits, and all the most fun activities scheduled as tightly as possible. Sure, moms still knock out the boring, messy, behind the scenes stuff, but the goal is to hurry through those insignificant moments as quickly as possible in order to get to the good stuff. You know, the social media post-worthy, good stuff. And, all the seasoned moms say in unison, 'Bless her heart.' That's southern for, "Poor girl." Like I said, that was what I thought...before I was a mom.

So, when I got married in my mid-thirties, became a stepmom to my three covenant kids, and became a mom to my daughter a year and a half later, I realized I had much to learn. Do you remember the scene in the movie, Finding Nemo, when they get sucked into the current the turtles were traveling in, being flipped around continuously? That's a rather accurate description of this season of my life. I felt swept into the fast-moving current of daily needs...schedule of others, endless chores, car rider lines, practices, sports, bottles and diapers, laundry and laundry and laundry. Toto, we're not in Kansas anymore, and this didn't look like the journey of motherhood I'd seen all those years before becoming a mom, myself.

Without realizing it, my *pre-motherhood* expectation of motherhood hindered how I was experiencing my *actual* motherhood journey. I placed the blue ribbon of importance on what I could offer my kids through organized, scheduled moments, and the other mom 'stuff' was just gap fillers that fell in between. Doing, more than being.

You may recognize how you've determined some of the 'blue ribbon' parenting instances in your own life by the moments you actually wash your hair and put on make-up. Or by the moments you take the picture and post it. Or better yet, you stage the moment specifically for the post. Yes, we tend to think 'those' moments are the moments that matter. Or at least I had as a new mom. All the other thousands of moments in between didn't carry the same value or significance in my children's lives or in my life as a mom. We'll call them mundane moments for this chapter.

Mundane moments can feel lonely, thankless, and never-ending. Exhaustion becomes a regular companion. There were times within this year I found myself feeling invisible, discouraged, and if I'm honest, a little resentful. At times, more than just a little. I wasn't even sure why. To top it off, I'd then feel guilty for feeling resentful. It was my first encounter with mom guilt. I was a first-time mom to a newborn and a new stepmom to three children with busy schedules. I loved the Lord, loved my daughter, and knew God was working in our blended family to redeem every heart and create real bonds between us. Still, I was aware of this internal tug of war and I was constantly asking God for help. It's not how I wanted to live any season of motherhood, or any season of life, for that matter. Struggling...then feeling guilty for struggling. It was a one-two punch.

There's a cornfield in our community God used to free me from this season of struggle. This cornfield sits right inside a winding curve in our neighborhood. At the end of summer, when the corn stalks are the highest, right before being harvested, vision is blinded around that curve. The irony of God using a blind curve to reveal my blinded perspective is not lost on me. He's just so creative like that.

The next spring, the same land sprouted different leaves. It's not noteworthy to the people in my town, but I was new to this farming community and I was awestruck. It was supposed to be a cornfield. I asked everyone I could about it, only to learn how purposeful it is to rotate crops on the same soil every few years. What had been a corn field was now a bean field. Mind blown.

Clearly, I'm no farmer. I can barely keep patio plants alive. I wish I could, but I can't. So, there's that. You see, (if you're a farmer or gardener, bear with me) soil needs different crops planted periodically, in order to replenish nutrients drained from it during prior seasons. Planting different crops promotes the richest soil, thus the richest harvest. So simple, (and apparently very common knowledge) yet fascinating to me.

During the same spring, I was on a walk with my newborn and I found myself at the edge of that field. Staring out across that field, asking God for help to break me out of this struggle I'd been wrestling with for about a year, I heard Him whisper in my heart, "Are you going to let Me grow a different crop in you?" I understood in an instant He was talking about the battle in my mind.

Sometimes God teaches us lessons at a patient, steady pace so we can learn in small doses as we go. Other times, He knows we need a right now, eye-opener kind of lesson. This was one of those right now lessons for me. It was instant, yet full of grace. It was as if He was gently taking my chin and turning it up toward His face to say, "We just need to reset your focus back to me. It's that simple."

I love the Lord deeply and sincerely, but I hadn't been loving Him with my mind. My thoughts had been spending way too much time on unrealistic expectations of what I thought life was going to look like, unrealistic expectations of myself in my new role, and it was warping my perspective. Even though my heart was longing for help, my mind was trying to figure it out on my own. God revealing that truth to me was all it took for a breakthrough. Immediate release. I can't explain to you in one chapter how something so simple changed everything for me, but it did. It was so simple, in fact, a few months later during my quiet time with the Lord, I laughed as I asked Him, "Lord, if that's all it took, why not just give me that nudge a little sooner? We could've wrapped up that season of struggling a little faster." Does anyone relate? When God's timing seems to extend a little longer than we hoped? Here's how He answered, "Because, Kyleen, I needed you to learn, bone deep, the importance of keeping your mind, not just your heart, set on Me."

The thief comes to steal, kill and destroy. Satan's relentless, but he's not creative. He's the author of lies, which means that's how he comes after us. Lies. And where could a lie do the most harm? His lies are aimed straight at our thought life. This kind of thinking can steal joy, kill connection with others, and destroy a life of purpose God's placed in every single moment in our homes. Moms, we don't have to take the bait.

The good news is God's given us every single thing we need to overcome a perspective problem and find God-size meaning and joy in the everyday calling of motherhood. This means we have a choice. We can refuse to become a FOMO (fear of missing out) mom, ranking our moments based on what culture says. Instead we can become a fearless mom. A faithful mom. When we lay down our expectations and find our identity in Christ, He'll shift our vision. That holy shift changes everything. We start to see *all* the parts of motherhood in an exciting way and find joy even in the moments that seemed pointless before. He grows contentment where resentment has been. Yes, even with laundry. Okay, maybe not laundry. But, stick with me. I want to share three things we need in our mom toolbelt to help us experience meaning and joy in our lives; a Holy Perspective, Learned Contentment (being not doing - being His more than being Mom), and a Special Ops Mentality (be ready to share the hope within you).

## What I Know Now:

1. **Holy perspective**

Scripture has so much to tell us about the importance of a holy perspective, a fixed focus. As much as we may love God with our hearts, this is a matter of our minds. Jen Wilkin, a Bible teacher, once explained the great commandment in Matthew 22:23 this way, "Interestingly, the same verse that commands us to love God with our hearts also commands us to love him with all of our minds." To be faithful women, when it comes to Christ, we must have devoted minds, not just affectionate hearts. Knowing this, He explains again and again *how* to have a holy perspective and what's at stake.

- "Love the Lord your God with all your heart *and* with all your soul *and* with all your mind." (Matthew 22:37)

- "Set your mind on things that are above...." (Colossians 3:2)

- "Now set your mind and heart to seek the Lord your God." (1 Chronicles 22:19)

- "To set the mind on the flesh is death, but to set the mind on the Spirit is life and peace." (Romans 8:6)

- "...take every thought captive..." (2 Corinthians 10:5)

- "Fix your thoughts on Jesus the apostle and high priest…. (Hebrews 3:1)

- "Fix your thoughts on what is true and honorable and right and pure, and lovely, and admirable. Think about things that are excellent and worthy of praise." (Philippians 4:8)

- "Fix these words of mine in your hearts and minds." (Deuteronomy 11:18)

- "So we fix our eyes not on what is seen, but what is unseen…" (2 Corinthians 4:18)

- "…be transformed by the renewing of your mind." (Romans 12:2)

Set your mind. Fix your thoughts. It's time to make up our minds about our minds. This is where the battle is fought and won for meaning and purpose in our lives, no matter how adventurous or how invisible the task. We've already been given victory and a roadmap. We simply must choose. Tony Evans Bible Commentary says this about the matter, "Setting your mind is like choosing a television station. You can watch channel 5 or channel 8, but you can't watch channel "5-and-8"."[iv] Choose the channel of holy perspective.

## 2. Learned contentment

God's not telling us to obey just because. Although, He could. He's God. In His gracious pursuing love, He invites us to deeper intimacy with Him. Deeper understanding about Him. Deeper purpose through Him. He's revealing to us the beauty and peace of a fixed gaze upon Him, and the contentment and meaning which hinges on our surrendered effort. No more expectations in any role we may have. The role of motherhood, the role of wife, or boss or co-worker or ministry title. No more searching for identity by culture's standards, we have the fullness of joy because belonging to Christ is our wellspring. And He is enough. Let's look at some of the promises God's given us when we seek Him;

- "You will keep him in *perfect peace* whose mind is stayed on you, because he trusts in you." (Isaiah 26:3)

- "You make known to me the path of life; *in your presence there is fullness of joy*; at your right hand are pleasures forevermore." (Psalm 16:11)

- "Better is one day in your courts than a thousand elsewhere;" (Psalm 84:10)

Fullness of joy and perfect peace are ours when our focus is resting in the Lord. Let's also take a look back at our opening verse from the Apostle Paul in Philippians 4:11 and read a little further. "…for I have learned in whatever situation I am to be content. I know how to be brought low, and I know how to abound. In any and every circumstance, I have learned the secret of facing plenty and hunger, abundance and need. I can do all things through Christ who strengthens me." (Philippians 4:11-13)

Many of us may know Philippians 4:13, and some may even have beautiful floral Bible covers with this verse on the front. Let's not miss the context in which Paul's describing the 'all things' he can do. When he's brought low, he can endure with contentment because he knows God is his Sustainer. When he's facing plenty, he can receive it with humble grace, content in knowing God alone is his Provider. Circumstances didn't dictate how Paul experienced life. His trust in God did. What makes Paul's message about contentment all the more powerful is understanding he wrote it while in prison, from his jail cell. Friends, this is the power of perspective. Holy focus.

### 3. Special ops mentality

As perspective shifts, and vision becomes clear, contentment flourishes. There resides the special ops mentality. Consider Paul again. If you're not familiar with the man God chose to write most of the New Testament of the Bible, it's Paul. Before he was Paul, though, he had to go through a perspective shift of his own.

His former name was Saul, and his job was hunting and killing Christians. On one of his trips he was heading from one city to another, he encountered God, who lovingly blinded him physically for several days in order to help him gain his spiritual sight. A newfound trust in God. He then restored his sight once the eyes of his heart were clear. Again, the irony isn't lost on me. It was then He gave Saul his new name, Paul, and with this holy perspective and learned contentment in his relationship with Christ, Paul was ready. He became a man on a mission for the Lord.

Like Paul, when we commit to a holy perspective and learn contentment in Christ, our hearts are available for God to use, as women on a mission. Special ops moms. If that doesn't fill your life with renewed purpose, I don't know what could! We have a one-of-a-kind, special ops, spiritual assignment with our children. God's positioned us like no other person in their lives. The truth is, these assignments sprinkled throughout our children's lives are going to be found in those mundane moments we've been busy rushing through. It's no wonder the enemy wants to warp our perspective and distract us with thoughts of discouragement, is it? These are the very moments of awesome we've been longing for.

Before you fall into a performance trap, pressuring yourself to figure out what these moments are, let me encourage you. God is not asking us to figure this out on our own. He's asking us to simply be available for them. How can we be ready and available? Focus on Him. Learn contentment through Him. When you're fixed on Him, He'll open the eyes of your heart to see the mission in the mundane.

A personal example for me involves the beloved car rider line. For the longest time, we had a DVD player in our vehicle. Like most good multitasking moms, I'd pop in a movie for them to watch, and I'd make the most of the time by hopping on a phone call with a friend or co-worker. It had become somewhat of an autopilot experience, day in and day out. Jump in the car, start the movie, head to school, make a call.

God gently reminded me of the treasure inside these before and after school car rides. Years before, car rider lines became the place my teenagers would unleash with all the chatter about their day; the drama at school, relationships, grades, the highs and the lows. It became a place where their teenage wall was down, and we connected in such a real way. It was also the place they were open to the drip of discipleship as we talked through whatever it was they were sharing. Years later, with my youngest one beginning school, God brought that to mind, so I took the DVD player out. Yes, at first, my daughter kept asking for it or saying she missed it. It wasn't long before we were singing songs on our drive or I'd hear about what the latest news was from elementary school. She'd blurt out random thoughts like little kids do, which turned into random thoughts about God, which turned into asking about knowing Him personally. We sat in the parking lot of her school one cold morning before drop off and prayed together. I would've missed it. God had a special ops assignment tucked inside that one more time, yesterday's mascara, still in my PJ's, car ride to school. Full of meaning and mission and purpose and joy. Heaven grew that morning, in a messy car on the way to school.

## Walking It Out:

### Review

Set aside time to do some honest inventory about your mind and your thought life. The sharpest Special Ops agents know how to do a little reconnaissance. "Search me, O God, and know my heart: try me, and know my anxious thoughts;" (Psalm 139:23) God has created us for meaning and purpose, and He desires for us to experience abundant life that He's already given us. (John 10:10) Ask him to show you the areas of a perspective problem keeping you from living with contentment. He's faithful, honest, and gentle…and He's able. He'll help you set your mind on Him, our true peace.

### Renew & Reroute

Once you identify where toxic thoughts have been taking root, commit to developing a daily habit to renew your mind and reroute your thinking. We've gone over the instructions all through scripture telling us to keep our mind set and thoughts fixed on the Lord. We've looked at promises where God tells us He gives perfect peace (Isaiah 26:3) and fullness of joy (Psalm 16:11) to those who are focused on Him and in His presence. Here's *how*:

*Renew:* Spend time in God's Word. It doesn't have to be complicated or hours long; but knowing Him through His Word is the path to a heart full of joy and in love with Christ.

*Reroute:* Catch a toxic thought in the act and reroute it. Here's a practical way to reroute your mind when you find yourself dwelling on thoughts that stir up anything other than contentment. When God reveals them, and He will, reroute with these two simple words said aloud to the enemy who is baiting you with those discouraging thoughts...*Not worthy.*

Look again at Philippians 4:8 where it says to think about things that are excellent and *worthy of praise*. "Fix your thoughts on what is true and honorable and right and pure, and lovely, and admirable. Think about things that are excellent and *worthy of praise*" (Philippians 4:8) I practice this is my own life and I've seen the power of a simple habit to overcome discouraging thoughts from the enemy. I've found myself home alone all day, folding and hanging up laundry, lost in my thoughts, when God reveals that crossroads in my mind. My response? Tell the enemy nope, literally speak the words "not worthy" aloud, and turn on my favorite music playlist or call a girlfriend as a way to snap out of my own head. It may sound silly to say it out loud, but speaking the truth straight to the lies is powerful and Biblical. "Death and life are in the power of the tongue." (Proverbs 18:21) You've been given power. Speak it.

**Relish**

Enjoy what God is sure to show you about those mundane moments just waiting to explode with meaning for you. A holy perspective matters, a learned contentment is promised, and joy is yours for the taking as you fix your gaze on the only one worthy of praise, Jesus.

## Questions for Reflection:

1.  What areas do you feel the most discouragement or resentment in your season of motherhood?

    _____

    _____

    _____

    _____

2.  As you pray for God to search you and your thoughts, what is He teaching you about where your mind is focused? Is the channel of your mind fixed on Him?

    _____

    _____

    _____

    _____

3.  What are some truths you can use to reframe an area where you may have a perspective problem?

    _____

    _____

    _____

    _____

4. Where have you experienced God revealing meaning in seemingly mundane moments?

_____

_____

_____

_____


5. What is one verse you'd like to memorize?

_____

_____

_____

_____

## Closing Prayer:

*Father God, You're so holy and in You, there is fullness of joy. Thank You for gently showing me that my one calling is to be Yours. Thank You for searching my thoughts and helping me to focus on You. I pray You would give me Your perspective and reveal meaning in the seemingly mundane moments of motherhood. In Jesus' name, Amen.*

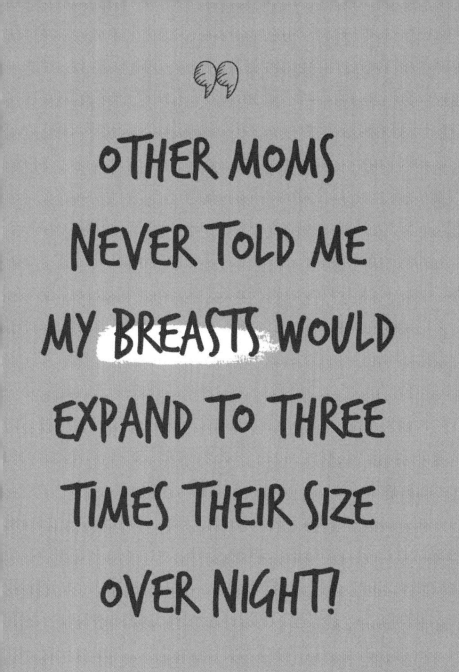

OTHER MOMS NEVER TOLD ME MY BREASTS WOULD EXPAND TO THREE TIMES THEIR SIZE OVER NIGHT!

MOMMENTOR.ORG

# Chapter 6

# Other Moms Never Told Me ...
## How to Extend Grace to Myself

*By Sarah Wood*

*...But He gives us more and more grace (through
the power of the Holy Spirit to defy sin and live an
obedient life that reflects both our family and
gratitude for our salvation). Therefore, it says,
"God is opposed to the proud and haughty, but
(continually)
gives (the gift of) grace to the humble
(who turn away from self-righteousness.)"*
*James 4:6 AMP*

I love singing. Now, if I'm being honest, I can't hold a note, but I love it all the same. Some of my specialties are Old Mac Donald, Happy Birthday, and that classic, Twinkle Twinkle. It does my ego a favor when one of my littles asks me to sing to them before bed. They love all the classics, but their favorite? Jesus Loves Me. A simple and sweet diddy, loved by countless. However, I think they love more than just the catchy tune and rhymes. I think they love the lyrics that hold the sweet comfort of knowing Jesus loves us above it all. The day behind them may have come with tantrums, time-outs, and their own poor choices, but when they hear that song, they gaze at me like their missteps never happened. They receive full forgiveness and grace without wrestling with guilt. No matter what the day brought before them, they are resting and comforted to sleep by my love and Jesus' love for them. They don't rest in guilt, condemnation, or shame. They rest in His love, knowing they are loved and filled with grace for a new day, the next morning.

Oh sigh.

Yet, me? I am still thinking about that bump I had when I overreacted in the car earlier.

## I Didn't See That Coming:

Adjusting to life with three kids was a whole new ball game for us.

Our precious toddler is active and keeps us on our toes. The two older, in elementary school, have full sports and activity schedules. Therefore, we run a tight ship with little wiggle room for the spontaneous. A system for everything and for everything a system.

I was feeling especially stretched one fall afternoon. On the way to soccer practice, I had a lot on my mind. I was bringing snacks for the team - *do I have enough ice in the cooler to keep the drinks cold?* I had to do countless things for my small group by the end of the week. I needed to order food from the grocery pickup soon. And I had to make an important phone call that evening. (The system thing, remember?)

My 6-year-old asked questions while my mind was full of my own to-do list...

"Who will be at practice?"

"Will I have someone to play with?"

"How long will it be?"

"Can we have Chick-fil-A tonight? I don't want crockpot dinner ..."

My 8-year-old chimed in too now...

"Mom, by the way, I need a new ball. Mine is too small, and I can't use this size. I need it nowwwww because my coach said I do."

Back to my six-year-old who screamed, "I was TALKING!"

And that woke up the baby....

Well, that did it. I snapped. I yelled.

"I just need a minute of quiet!" I shouted. "Just hush!"

Bursts of tears from them. Shame from me. Ugh. Now, I'm not a yeller normally, but today was just too much, and unfortunately, my family paid the heavy price of my reactions. I wish I could say the rest of the evening went well, but it didn't. I proceeded to be grumpy all through practice and all the way home. This led to the domino effect in the house, and now everyone was cross. Then, because I was upset at myself for upsetting everyone else, I spent the rest of the evening frustrated. That night, I walked the kids to brush teeth, read stories and sing. Before putting them each to bed, I apologized. They smiled, and quickly forgave me, giggling…they already forgot about it. But I hadn't. I didn't like feeling pushed to the edge and I certainly didn't want to live the guilt of my emotional car eruption all night long.

Have you been there? You know the drill.

- When you have so much on your mind that you burst into tears when you can't find your keys.

- When you overreact to a comment your husband made, and snap at him.

- When your to-do list is miles long and find yourself having a short fuse with everyone…including the innocent lady at the Starbucks drive-thru.

- When your kids are fighting, you have things to get done, so you yell at them, like they have a personal mission to derail you from your achievements.

When I flopped into the bed that night, feeling crummy, I looked at my husband and asked what I did wrong. He smiled, prayed for me, and shared that God's mercies are new every morning. (He's a keeper.) As we shut off the light, and went to sleep, my thoughts began to take shape. At first, it was the nagging feeling of wishing the evening went better. Why did it have to end in frustration? Then, the Lord told me our routines actually can go better. And most of the change needed to start…with me.

Ouch.

Now, at this point my mind can go into two different paths. Condemnation or conviction? One unleashes hope, and the other failure. One is filled to the brim with grace…the other, a continued cycle of self-inflicting pain. I know I want to be better equipped to handle these stressful moments. I know that's what God wants for me. I wanted my capacity for life's circumstances to grow, just like Paul in Philippians 4, who was content with a little or a lot. Yet, in the days that followed, my mind swirled with thoughts and feelings of inadequacy. The Lord had spoken to me that what I did was wrong, but now what?

I felt ill-equipped to control my own stress and worried I would be unable to stop my feelings and therefore, my mouth, the next time. And Lord knows, there will be plenty of next times. As the mind-swirling settled, I identified three natural thought processes on how I was coping with the events of the week before. Although these processes are common, they are not answers to how God wants to equip us to receive His grace and move forward.

## False Processes

**Rationalizing:** First, I tried to rationalize my behavior because, "Well, I'm tired! I do a lot! It's okay as long as I apologize and show my kiddos I was wrong!" Nice try, but it didn't soothe. I knew God's promises and what the fruit of the Spirit is. I hadn't operated in them. I was operating in impatience, selfishness, and frustration. So, rationalizing my behavior based on circumstances is not the truth.

**Shame:** Second, I tried to condemn myself through the lens of shame. The thoughts were, "This is just how you are. You can't change. You're just a bad mom." This was even worse! This isn't of Jesus. Condemnation is the language of the enemy and actually causes us to identify with the lies of the enemy. The enemy calls you these false names, and when I give merit to these thoughts, I choose to partner with him. God does not call us this, therefore shaming my behavior is not the truth.

**False agreement:** And thirdly, I called a friend and confessed and she kindly said, "Aw, it's okay, we all have our moments." Yes, now this felt better.  However, it didn't give me any hope next time would yield a life-giving result, and I truly do want to respond better next time. While I appreciate the grace from my friend, I can easily fall into the false agreement that leads me back to rationalizing!

There is a popular thought process that tells us we have a "right" to these feelings and it's okay to have moments where we come apart at the seams. While I believe they are natural, I do not believe God wants to leave us there repeating the same cycle. He desires for us to be Spirit led, and not be led by our flesh and circumstances. He desires for us to be more like Him. My friend wasn't wrong, we all do have our moments. However, agreeing that our kids deserve this, or I deserve to lose it, is not the truth.

You may recognize or even identify with one of the three, or even all of them at one time or another. Our culture often uses these thoughts to try and give our tired souls a salve that will not satisfy. I had entertained each of these thought processes for far too long and knew these were not in the Word of God. In fact, many of them are direct opposites to what God would have us do. I was ready to hear and walk in His truth.

## What I Know Now:

*"There is no condemnation for those in Christ Jesus."*
*Romans 8:1*

I read the words of Romans 8 and realized that continuing any of the above processes would not allow me to grow past these recurring moments of frustration. I want to set a more joyful and peaceful tone in my home. I wanted to do things God's way and live by His truth, but I needed tools to get there. I plunged myself into quiet time before God to plead for help in this area. I knew it was possible, and not only that, I knew it was what God desired for me and our family.

Before the sun came up one early morning, the Lord revealed to me that it is grace. God has called us righteous because of the completed work of Jesus on the cross. He extends His grace and forgiveness to us and I received it when I chose to invite him into my life to be my Savior. Yet, because I was dwelling on my mistake, I was actually withholding His grace and forgiveness by condemning myself. He died to set me free. Why was I punishing myself? Instantly I thought of my children, nestling in their beds to the song, Jesus loves me. They didn't bring up that time they smacked their brother. They didn't bring up that one time they colored on the walls.

They rested in His grace and love. They moved forward, forgiven, grace-filled, and loved. His grace and love cover every and all sin. Not only does God's grace wash us clean as snow, it actually empowers us to do His will. It is impossible for us to counteract the frustration and selfishness that arise when life's wild circumstances come at us. His grace is actually strength and empowerment to turn from my natural responses into what His Spirit desires for me. And friends, let me tell you, He desires good for you. The Lord has called me to many things. He has called me to be a mom. He has called me to be a wife to my husband. He has called me to serve and love others. And because I am called, I know He will empower me to walk in those callings, if I allow Him to do this beautiful, holy work. This is grace. The empowerment, strength and forgiveness to be like Jesus in all areas where He leads me.

## Walk It Out:

Being a follower of Christ, is just that. We follow Christ. It's the willingness to lay our lives down and allow Him to fill us with His Spirit and exchange our perspectives for His. We read Scripture and ask God to renew our minds and hearts, to align ourselves with His Word, not our own desire and perception. While I am weak and have complaining moments, I'm asked by Jesus to acknowledge my missteps. I've been created to take them to Him and allow Him to clean the "yuck" out my heart. It takes faith as we trust Him to reveal the selfishness, bitterness, and anything else that creeps in and causes short fuses.

Ephesians 4 and 1 Thessalonians 2 are two examples in Scripture of God's promise to help us on our quest to be more like Him. They open the conversation that God has created us for more than just a day's work. It's the notion that we are called to something greater than ourselves and our own comfort. It's the plea of Paul to us as Christ followers to allow Jesus to do a work in us and not leave us as we are. It's a brave, "Yes," to allow God to work in our hearts and remove the impurities that hurt ourselves and others. It is only then, we will truly walk freely, worthy of the calling in which He has called us. This is not a works based worthy. It's a grace-rooted worthy, one that knows if we allow Him to purify our hearts and cleanse us of selfishness, He is faithful to use us for His glory. His way is better. His way is *truth.* And I choose to lose my life so I may find it. It's in these vulnerable times, when His Word becomes *alive.* Not only are we reading it, but it will transform us and yield a fruitful shift in our lives and our homes.

The short answer, mama, is there *is* hope.

So, where do we go from here? We need a practical battle plan to slough the shame off and receive the grace so freely given to us.

## 1.  Acknowledge wrongdoing...and where it's from.

This is a first step and this one can sting a little. Another word for this is humility. We recognize we aren't perfect and need Jesus to show us where, and how to help heal our hearts and brokenness. This also requires some background work into the "why." "Why did I explode on my daughter for asking simple questions?" There are various "reasons," but we must be careful to identify them, and not use them as a crutch to blame or rationalize. This will require us to go before God in quiet time and ask Him to show us all areas where we are angry, stressed, etc. It's not fun, and it's not pretty, but I promise He is faithful to do this work. He sees all of you, and still loves you so there isn't anything you can hide.

Some examples may be:

- Feeling overwhelmed and busy

- Tired/hungry

- Saying directions more than once

- Schedule is too rigorous without flexibility

Once you've identified some of the triggers, it can help you work through the difficult moments that pop up during your day. My pastor's wife, Emily, shared with me that often the brokenness in us can cut others if we are left without asking God for His grace. It's important to allow Him to truly examine our hearts before we can walk into the next step.

> *"Search me, God and know my heart; test me and*
> *know my anxious thoughts. See if there is any*
> *offensive way in me, and lead me in the way*
> *everlasting."*
> *Psalm 139:23-24*

## 2. Repent.

The act of repentance is the decision to not only acknowledge our shortcoming and missteps, but to make the decision that we don't want to act that way anymore. We tell God we repent, and we don't want to react like that again.

Truly decide you don't want to have that bitterness, malice, ungratefulness, etc. in your heart. It's not God's best for us. **But also, don't be disheartened…this is not a call to be "well behaved." This is a call to be humble before Jesus and tell Him, we need help!**

> *"Those who belong to Christ Jesus have nailed the*
> *passions and desires of their sinful nature*
> *to his cross and crucified them there."*
> Galatians 5:24

### 3. Don't let shame tempt you.

I'm sure you've heard those little voices in your head replaying the scenario over and over (and over). This is not of God! This is shame and shame is sneaky. Remember, you are human and each of us needs help to navigate this world. Shame wants to keep you feeling guilty so you can never grow. If the enemy can keep you in the cycle of shame, you won't recognize the truth of what God says about you. We must forgive ourselves and stand on His promises. We will extend grace to ourselves and allow God to renew our minds and cleanse our hearts. You're not a terrible mom, you had a terrible moment. But you have God. Speak words of *life* over yourself and the situation.

*"Those who look to Him for help will be radiant with joy; no shadow of shame will darken their faces."*

*Psalm 34:5*

*"For I will be merciful toward their iniquities, and I will remember their sins no more."*

*Hebrews 8:12*

*"No, dear brothers and sisters, I have not achieved it, but I focus on one thing: Forgetting the past and looking forward to what lies ahead."*

*Philippians 3:13*

## 4. Read Scripture and meditate on it.

This means you are exchanging those negative thoughts or shame thoughts with God's truth. Every time a thought of shame or condemnation comes into your mind, you stop it and focus on the Word of God. You can build an arsenal of verses in your journal or take some from this chapter to stand on when you feel yourself slipping back into a pit. Never underestimate the value of memorizing scripture.

*"All Scripture is God-breathed and is used for*
*teaching, rebuking, correcting, training in*
*righteousness,*
*so that the servant of God may be thoroughly*
*equipped for every good work."*
*2 Timothy 3:16-17*

## 5. Rejoice!

You've just been given an opportunity for growth. This
may not feel good, but it is good. When God removes
impurities from your life, He wants His Spirit and its fruit to
grow in its place. Ask God to fill you with joy and
thankfulness instead or selfishness and anger. We aren't just
repenting and turning from our ways, but we are actually being
filled by the Holy Spirit. One thing that helped me was to keep
a list each day of things that brought me joy, (No, no, not
sparked joy...) and that I am thankful for. This will help your
mind to focus on the good He brings you.

*"But the Holy Spirit produces this kind of fruit in*
*our lives: love, joy, peace, patience, kindness,*
*goodness, faithfulness, gentleness, and self-control."*
*Galatians 5:22*

## 6. Take a break.

Okay mamas. I have a new saying and it's this...screen time is better than scream time. I'm no doctor, but I will tell you this, sometimes you need a minute. You need a few moments with God to get your head and heart aligned with Him again. And that is *okay*. Throw on a half hour show for the littles and lay down on the floor in a quiet space. Ask him for His grace. If you draw close to Him, He will draw close to you. He is faithful to shower His love all over you...and by the time Paw Patrol is over, I promise.

*"God is our refuge and strength, an ever present*
*help in times of trouble."*
*Psalm 46:1*

As you are reading, you may be wondering if this is a perfect and foolproof plan. Oh friend, no. I can tell you there are (and will be) times again when I fall short. I have yelled and probably will yell again. I caught myself complaining again and raced to the thankfulness scriptures I have plastered on the wall. However, I have hope that whenever I fall short, it is not who I am. Let's refuse to wear the shame of it. Let's give ourselves grace and run straight to God to repent, rather than try and self-soothe with words that aren't His. Declare His Words over your situation, and He is faithful to meet us where we are at…with His grace in abundance.

## Questions for Reflection:

1. Is anger/frustration a go-to response for you? Is this what Jesus calls us to?

_____

_____

_____

_____

2. How do you cope with a rough day or moment?

_____

_____

_____

_____

3. Do you tend to condemn yourself if you fall short? His grace is made perfect in our weakness!

_____

_____

_____

_____

4. What are some scriptures you can stand on to bring joy into your situation?

_____

_____

_____

_____


5. Is receiving God's grace easy for you? Why or why not?

_____

_____

_____

_____

## Closing Prayer:

*Lord, I thank You that You have called me to be a mother to my children. You have not only called me to this, but You have anointed me for this work. I submit myself and my parenting to You. I ask You, Lord, to give me the strength, power, and creativity to guide my children in all areas of their lives. I know I cannot do this in my own ability. Lord, empower me, and give me Your grace when and where I fall short. I pray You give me the nudge to do things YOUR way. I pray when I do make a misstep, that Your love and grace cover me and my family. In Jesus name, Amen.*

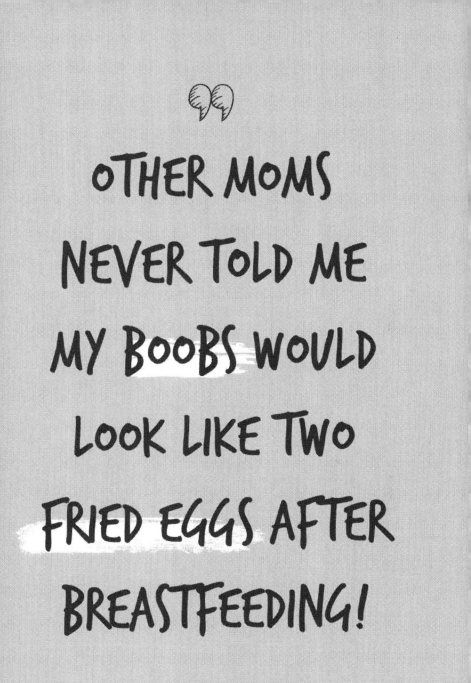

OTHER MOMS
NEVER TOLD ME
MY BOOBS WOULD
LOOK LIKE TWO
FRIED EGGS AFTER
BREASTFEEDING!

Chapter 7

# Other Moms Never Told Me ...
# How to Love Hard AND Fight Hard

*By Chris Blue*

*"...with honey from the rock, I would satisfy you."*
*Psalm 81:16*

## I Didn't See That Coming:

I stood on my front lawn and screamed when my daughter told me she was pregnant on a summer night before her senior year. One year later, I cried silent, uncontrollable tears as I withdrew my son from school and checked him into his first rehab.

I wore black on days like these since I was, after all, mourning the loss of so much.

It has been said that parenting toddlers is physically exhausting, but parenting teens is emotionally exhausting, and I wholeheartedly concur. John and I were just two people who fell in love and thought it would be fun to have some babies. What I didn't see coming was that God would use their teenage struggles to strengthen our family and drive me closer to Him.

I always knew I wanted to love big, but I didn't know I wanted a big family. When I met my husband, I danced for the Los Angeles Laker Girls, and he played hockey for the Boston Bruins. We were married in California and soon moved to Austin, Texas, to pastor a church. Retiring from professional sports to be in full-time ministry sounds like a logical progression, doesn't it? We heard the message of the Gospel, threw our hearts at Jesus like a hot potato, went all in and never looked back!

Everyone knows that everything's bigger in Texas, and that also applies to family, where the average size is at least four kids. McKennah, Jackson, Tennyson, and Hudson were all two years apart, and in my eyes, the most winsome brood on the block! Nine years later we moved back to Southern California to plant another church, and Georgia was born to nicely complete our family of seven. We quickly went from average to the anomaly, to whom no one wanted to live next door!

I feel like in those early years, I was never without a baby in me, on me, or around me. Our days were marked by parks, playtime, and Play-Doh. Our years would grow to include a plethora of sweet moments like soccer games and cupcake parties, chicken minis and pulling kids from class to apologize for a hard morning. However, neither *What to Expect When You're Expecting* nor *Growing Kids God's Way* prepared me for the night that would come.

Our daughter told us on a Friday evening, and I'm sad to admit that forgiveness and acceptance didn't come readily. Harsh and hurtful words were spoken, the kind that sting and are hard to take back. There was disappointment. There was death to so many dreams, and I did not grieve quietly. My Christianity seemed to go out the window while Fear and Judgement walked in the front door.

Relentless questions rolled in my head

*Did that purity ring not mean anything to her?*

*What was she missing that our family life didn't provide?*

*Were we wrong to open the door of hospitality and ministry to this boy?*

*What about school?*

*What about the baby?*

Our initial response was adoption. However, a wise man, who walked a similar path with his own daughter, encouraged us to hold off with, "You never know what God can do."

Early the following morning, after I exploded all over McKennah with every "You've ruined your life" sentiment a mother should never say, she crawled into my bed, curled up next to me almost child-like, and in all sincerity whispered, "You're such a hypocrite. My story is not over. This is just the beginning. What I have done may be wrong, but this baby will be a blessing. All day long we tell people how God restores, but you think there's no redemption for this baby?" She began to preach to me and speak life over her child.

The enemy will try to tell you you're disqualified as a parent, certainly from ministry, but this moment showed us that what we poured into her for years took root in her heart and was now springing up hope where I could only stir up despair.

Our family mantra has long been, "Love hard, fight hard." We are passionate people and have no reservations about expressing that passion through deep affection and heated conversation. No "passive aggressive, stuff-your-feelings" happening here. A week later, the crisis moment left us with hearts pounding, furrowed brows, and pulses racing but also ensured this baby would be a Blue. OB appointments were made, showers were planned, a nursery was designed, and at age 47, with four other young children at home, I became a Lala.

*Psalm 81:16 says, "I would feed you the finest wheat; with honey from the rock, I would satisfy you."*

We love the good gluten part but find it difficult to believe that sweetness could come from the hard. Charles Spurgeon said, "I have learned to kiss the wave that slammed me into the rock." Typically, we spend more time kicking, in hopes of getting some honey out of our heavy. But these days we clamor over who's the first to kiss this little piece of pure sunshine running up and down our halls! His mother is beautiful and brilliant and brings to the table of her generation that which is powerful and important and necessary. And what we once thought was tragic, God used as the very source of joy when our next storm hit.

I was in North Carolina for a writers' workshop when I got the call. It would be the first of multiple suicide attempts by our sixteen-year-old son. What we perceived to be teenage apathy was actually depression, with wrestlings much too deep to talk about here. We soon discovered Jack turned to drugs to numb, and a refusal to quit led to three years of more pain.

Our lives consisted of:

- Countless trips to the ER

- Stays in six psychiatric hospitals

- Local residential programs and out of state rehabs - some good, some terrible

- More therapy and medications, ambulance rides, and waiting rooms than I want to recall.

No one ever told me this baby with jaundice and respiratory problems would someday be addicted to a substance that was killing him. I learned how to love hard and fight hard at my son, Jack's bedside. Early 19th century theologian, Nathaniel William Taylor, once said, "A person who has experienced great difficulties will not be easily parted from his Bible." I camped out in the New Testament and curled up in Psalms. I wielded the Word over his room and his friends, begged prayers of trajectory-turning, and God showed up in tangible, life-giving ways.

Jack is magnetic, and people are drawn to his kindness. He will look you in the eye, ask you sincerely about your day, and you will walk away knowing the depths of the Father's love after spending even a moment with him. His mind is sharp, his penmanship impeccable, and the sound of his song ministers to those who would hear. He has been sober for a year and five months. Stung by the past, the sweetness of his redemption shines brighter. There is greatness all over him, and I can't wait to see what God will write next for his story.

## What I Know Now:

**1. You can do the thing you don't think you can do.**

Move houses.

Change jobs.

Lose jobs.

Get up, feed people, play with kids, do laundry, go to bed, repeat.

Homeschool.

Send them to school.

Hear the word and weight of your diagnosis.

Stand next to the casket of your toddler.

Fight for your marriage.

Fight to move on if it ends.

Sit in a boardroom all day and a living room all night.

Take your baby to college.

Step back while he strains through Statistics.

Watch your daughter become a teen mom.

Visit your son in rehab.

Rebuild after everything has burned away.

You can do it because God is already there in it.

Sometimes when the hard comes, it rolls in like a storm. Dust clouds billowing, hard rain stinging, thunder and lightning flashing overhead. We tend to turn and run away fervently from the chaos as if a tsunami is barreling through. But sometimes we need to stop dead in our tracks, turn around and face the ferocity of the fight. There may be a day when you have to dive into the disappointment, hold hands with the heartache, taste the pain, and linger in the layers of loss.

> Revelation 12:6 reads, *"The woman fled into the wilderness to a place prepared for her by God, where she might receive nourishment…"*.

Into the wilderness.

Prepared by God.

Where she might receive nourishment.

We're supposed to fight the good fight of faith, not fight the *faith*. When I stopped hiding from God and started fighting the right fight, things began to change. Like most women, I was a control freak, mostly because I worried what you would think of me. Out of fear and insecurity, I would try to control situations. I found myself in a stronghold of manipulation and unmet expectations as I struggled to juggle all the things to make sure none of the balls hit the ground. One day at a silent retreat while studying the names of God and reflecting on "Mighty God," the tune to the old cartoon, Mighty Mouse, came to mind. "Here I come to save the day!" In that moment, the Lord whispered to me, "I AM the one who saves the day, not you. Your rescue looks like enabling. Mine looks like salvation." When we stop running, turn and embrace the season we're in, we stop striving and contriving. We see that Jesus not only brings hope. He IS Hope.

## 2.  **God puts you into Himself.**

One of my life verses is found in Psalm 18:19, *"He brought me out into a spacious place; He rescued me because He delighted in me."* For years, I thought the Father was perpetually disappointed in me, but He's crazy about you and me! Do you know what the spacious place is? It's Himself. He doesn't pick you up and put you into a better situation necessarily. He doesn't take you from one marriage and put you into a different one, or give you a better house or children who perfectly obey, or answer every prayer to your liking. He puts you into Himself. A situation healed or a prayer heard is not the answer. HE is the answer. I once asked my husband a series of questions...

Will we ever be able to build a home again?

What's our next direction financially?

Will I ever write a book?

Will our son get sober?

He simply looked at me and said, "You're asking the wrong questions. The question should be, is Jesus enough?"

Are you familiar with the story of the adulterous woman told in John 8? A woman, naked and vulnerable, caught in the middle of her "hard", is standing before her accusers. Jesus stoops to write something on the ground and one by one, her enemies leave. I have always been absolutely fascinated by this...she stays. Can you imagine? You're in a precarious position and those who held stones to throw at you have now fled. We run away all the time. Why didn't she? When she had every opportunity to make her escape, why did she remain? She knew Jesus was enough.

She must have seen something in Jesus' eyes that changed her. She faced her pain and what was staring back at her was forgiveness and acceptance and love. She saw someone who stood for her, fought for her, believed in her, even in her foolishness. When we can be transparent enough to stand naked and vulnerable in front of Jesus, we can stand before men and women who pick up stones meant for us. When we have no need to wear masks or hide…when we can face the pain of what we fear and that which we cannot control, then we have something authentic people can believe in. We can know He is enough for our situations, giving us connection with Him and those around us, which is essential in loving and fighting hard.

3. **You're not alone.**

One day, when we were in the heart of our hard, I went to get my nails done. Two women were next to me, and one was loudly exclaiming how she had turned her garage into a hangout space in an attempt to keep her kids out of trouble, specifically from teenage pregnancy and drugs. I had so much to say but remained quiet as I admired the other woman's darling shoes. Oddly, she was silent too.

When my freshly painted nails and I got up to leave, I stopped to smile and say, "I love your cute shoes!" I thought of her so many times throughout the rest of the day. Her somber demeanor. Her super pretty short haircut. Her shy smile. And those shoes. Later that evening when it was time for rehab visiting hours, I was playing a round of cards with my son when I glanced across the room and locked my stare on a pair of shoes that looked eerily familiar. My eyes met hers with a knowingness that needed no words. We both had kids the same age who were hurting. We both spent our evenings in a psychiatric lobby. We were both just trying to maintain a sense of normalcy in a salon. We were quiet that morning for a reason. The same reason. It was nice to meet someone who was tired of juggling the balls that lay on the ground around her too.

The enemy is crafty, but he's not creative. The story of the Bible from beginning to end is one of reconciliation. Your enemy knows he can never be reconciled to the Father so he will do whatever it takes to separate and isolate you from Him and from one another. God's plan is always togetherness. Connection is rooted in authentic vulnerability.

C.S. Lewis defined it best when he said, "Friendship is one person saying to the other, 'What, you too? I thought I was the only one.'"[v] Transparency in shared experiences opens doors, but it's the Spirit of God who does the true work of connection because it's about reminding another that He is for them! Jesus was the greatest Friend because He stayed connected to the Father. So, as you love hard and fight hard, continue to look up, but also look around, 'cause you never know when the Lord will use some fabulous shoes to lift your blues!

**Walking It Out:**

### 1. Don't compare your hard to another's.

I'll never forget walking with a heavy-hearted friend one day. She was deeply puzzled as she said, "I just don't know where he's going to go, Pepperdine or Vanderbilt." She was referring to her high school senior as he neared graduation, the same age as my son. What I wanted to say was, "You're trying to figure out where your son is going to college, and I'm just hoping mine lives another day." But you can't do that. That's not fair. That's her difficult place, and it might not seem as grave as yours, but it's still hard. One day your seasons might be reversed, so ask God to give you a "periscope perspective."

Remember the periscope is the device positioned at the top of a submarine, which allows the observer to see things otherwise out of sight. Too often we are like patrons of a parade. We only see the float directly in front of us. We don't know where the marching band is, when the horses are going to poop, or if Santa is the big finale. God sees from beginning to end, and we cannot fathom all He has for us. Have grace for someone else, even if their hard seems sweeter than yours.

## 2. Remind yourself of His faithfulness.

Psalm 63 tells of David hiding out in desert caves. *"God, You are my God. I eagerly seek You. I thirst for You. My body faints for You in a land that is dry, desolate and without water. So I gaze on you in the sanctuary to see your strength and glory."* David's in a dark and dry place, but he remembers what he saw in the sanctuary. He's reminding himself in the hard what he tasted in the sweet. He is taking what he gleaned from a sanctuary on Sunday into his circumstances on Monday.

I declare and decree all the time that we will "have no fear of bad news" (Psalm 112:7), that we will "see the goodness of the Lord in the land of the living" (Psalm 27:13), and we recount the countless times we have seen God show His faithfulness on our behalf. See, you may have been marked by the hard, but you are not defined by it. Only Jesus gets to do that.

### 3. Shift the atmosphere.

Did you ever see the movie, Bring It On? In one scene, the cheerleaders chant, "BRRRR, IT'S COLD IN HERE. THERE MUST BE A CLOVER IN THE ATMOSPHERE." At some point the cheerleader in you has to rise up and call for a shift in the atmosphere. The wilderness place from Revelation 12 was prepared for the woman's nourishment, not her detriment. When you begin to understand that your hard isn't meant to destroy you, but to grow you, your perspective begins to change. You can shift from fear mode to faith mode, embrace this season and see how the Lord would hone you in this hardened place.

There's a shift not only in the way you view the crisis, but in the way you handle the chaos. We used to escalate and emotionally react in our house. Now we try to wisely respond. Our words were once sprinkled with cynicism. Now they're seasoned with grace again. We spent nights running from conflict. Now we race toward restoration. God is not moved off His throne the way you are thrown by this move. His stripping may feel like ripping, but He is shaping you for a calling.

There is something you are supposed to do that you couldn't do before because you didn't have access. The wilderness waterfall you endure grants you access. When we remember that a waterfall pounds down but also pushes out, then you can know that this thing isn't meant to drown you but to propel you. Access Granted.

Our story is about unconditional love. Never giving up on anyone ever. Steadfastness over the long haul. We know what it is to love hard, fight hard, stay in the ring and show up for the ones who matter because we have had to do it for each other. We have seen Jesus firsthand chase us down with His love, and we have lived out the lyrics of shadow-lighting and mountain-climbing. Your struggles don't have to be this traumatic. Even small things can feel weighty. But no matter the size, lean into the Lord. Allow your heart to be honed and grown in the hard. I promise, you will taste the sweet from the bitter.

## Questions for Reflection:

1. Where are you in the stages of hard? In denial? Embracing your circumstances?

_____

_____

_____

_____

2. What are you trying to control? Can you see where you are enabling or co-dependent in a situation?

_____

_____

_____

_____

3. How do you typically respond to the hard? Hide, run away or stay?

_____

_____

_____

_____

4. Where do you need an atmospheric shift?

_____

_____

_____

_____

5. If this is not your story, do you know someone on a similar journey who could use encouragement?

_____

_____

_____

_____

## Closing Prayer:

*Father, Your Word says You are a good God, and You give good gifts. I choose to trust You even when I don't see You in my storm. May I dig deep and find the footing of my faith in this season. Don't let me take the reins of control from Your hands. Help me not to be marked by worry but stand on Your Word. Strip away, that Your presence may be more palpable. I bind fear and hopelessness in the name of Jesus, and I declare my deliverance and receive the peace You breathe upon me. Strengthen my rest and resolve. I ask You would pull out every bit o' honey from every bite of hard, that I may be a deep well holding untainted waters, which others may come and find refreshment for their parched souls.*

*Light and not darkness. Joy and not sadness. Hope and not despair. Life and not death.*

*In the powerfully powerful, yet sweetly near name of Jesus, Amen and amen.*

OTHER MOMS NEVER TOLD ME I WOULD MOST LIKELY POOP WHILE I PUSHED IN LABOR!

# Chapter 8

# Other Moms Never Told Me ...
# Parenting Is Forever

*By Rhonda Ihrig*

*"... for He Himself has said, 'I will never desert*
*you, nor will I ever forsake you,'"*
*Hebrews 13:5*

## I Didn't See That Coming:

I grew up as an only child and as a "closet romantic." I
enjoy movies where love prevails and I read novels where in
the midst of tragedy, love wins out. So, when I got married,
that is what I thought life would be. I anticipated living a big
romantic movie. I was sure it would play out like a great novel,
with everything perfect, and with beautifully dressed children
quietly reading in a tufted chair. It was going to be the makings

of a fairy tale, perfectly packaged. Well, as you can imagine, it didn't happen the way I saw it in the movies!

My husband, Larry, and I dated, got married, went on a brief honeymoon, then real life happened. I didn't see it coming. We had been married about two years when our daughter, Gina, was born. Up until then my life was still pretty smooth and most things were to my liking. Larry was in ministry, and quite busy, so I could still go shopping *alone,* do housework *alone,* read a book *alone*, and sew *alone*. But when we brought our daughter home from the hospital, I felt instantly overwhelmed. I had no time to myself, no time to regroup, and hardly a second to recharge. If you're a mom, you know the routine…feeding every 2-4 hours, changing cloth diapers, (yeah, you heard me… <u>cloth</u> diapers), rocking her to keep her calm, and doing just about anything to get her to sleep.

Gina started talking at 12 months old (it's the truth). Her first sentence was, "Oooh, what dat?" Her venture into linguistics was a question designed for engagement. From that day forward she did not demonstrate any desire to stop communicating. Because I was an only child, Gina's free-flow of words was something I didn't see coming. I wanted a few moments of silence but found none. It's not that she was an undisciplined, out-of-control child. She was just given an abundance of words and needed to use them all, everyday. "Mommy read me", "mommy play with me", "mommy watch me', "mommy come here", "look mommy", "mommy I wanna go Tao (Taco) Bell." Gina didn't have a slow down or mute button. Believe me, I looked! And when Gina started to walk, she was everywhere...quickly. Keeping up with her felt like marathon training, and I've never had any desire to run recreationally.

When my husband asked about having a second child, it was out of the question. I think I actually asked him, "Are you nuts?!" Some of you understand that feeling and some of you may not. But I was just too worn out. I really did love being a mom, I just felt that that I would not survive an additional encounter. Fortunately, I started to adapt to my newly defined "fairy tale life" and when our daughter turned 2 ½, we had our second child.

Our son, Brent, had a completely different personality. He was quiet, seemed really relaxed, played well by himself, and as he began to grow, didn't have much to say. Actually, he didn't need to say much because his big sis was willing to do most of the talking for him. She was large and in charge and as long as he was the smaller of the brood, he went along with it.

His early life was simple--if he was full at one end and clean at the other, he was good. After a very active, constantly engaging, always moving little one, I wasn't sure what to do with a quiet, sedentary child. There were times I wouldn't hear anything from him for an hour or more. I'd go to his room, find him lying on the floor, staring at a line of perfectly parked matchbox cars, seeming entranced by the wonders of his ability to create such beauty. I couldn't fully grasp his demeanor but certainly appreciated it.

As our children grew, each stage of their life revealed new and different things about them. School work came naturally to Gina, while Brent seemed to work harder at it. They both were very good athletes. Gina was a JO (Junior Olympic) swimmer and Brent was a football CIF champion and all-star. Though they each had some defined moments of challenge as teenagers, for the most part, they were pretty great kids.

So, when they, in turn, had their 18th birthday, I thought my parenting days were over. They both married in the same year (2000), one in February and one in December. Larry and I had become empty nesters and it was a relief to think that our parenting days were behind us. They were on their own, supporting themselves, and creating their own journey. We were enjoying our freedom. Until, one afternoon my husband

and I came home to their cars parked in our driveway. That was the clue they were gathered in our house. And when we walked in the front door, we found them, all of them, laying on the floor, and sprawled on the couches in our family room, the TV blaring, and postured like a planned take-over.

Now we enjoyed visits from time to time, but I didn't see this coming. And to add to the unplanned surprise, when we walked through the door, they all asked, "What's for dinner mom?" It wasn't, "Hi mom and dad. We love you!" or "We love what you've done with the place!" or "We have been thinking about you guys and wanted to come by to see how you were doing!" We obviously had different definitions of what "on your own" meant. If you're broke, you have no food in your place, and payday isn't for two days, mom and dad will rescue you. My first thought was, "Wait a minute! We have a life, and you have a life! You know...our house, your house, our stuff, your stuff, our time, your time." But the look on their faces made me realize I was not done parenting. I may have thought the apron strings were cut, but I knew in my heart the apron of motherhood fit me well, and I liked it. From that day forward our house remained a place to hang out, get a meal, play games, celebrate, and live life together. Measured parenthood continued and that was okay.

Several years later the Lord directed my husband and I to pastor a church about a 7-hour drive away. None of us saw this coming. Up to this point our family never lived farther than a few miles from each other. This move came as an absolute shock to our extended family, but most shocking to our children. It was even more difficult when my husband told them we were going, but they couldn't go with us. You see, we knew God had called us, and if it was His will for them to join us, He *might* eventually call them. The request we made of them was to wait on God, trust His lead, and to not make any life-altering moves for at least a year. That would give God a season to clarify His plan for them.

We had always raised our kids to know the voice and direction of the Lord and this was their biggest opportunity to put that to the test. Immediately following us would have been the direction of their emotions, not the direction of the Spirit. As God spoke to us about moving, in time the Spirit might lead them our direction. This was one of the more difficult decisions Larry and I ever made, but our children honored our request. And one year to the day, our daughter, son-in-law, and new grandson arrived at our house. They knew their move was directed by the Lord, and having a child of their own, they wanted parents to help them parent. It was a high honor to help because I remember panicking when I had my first child and really had no idea what to do. I was blessed enough to have a mother-in-law to rescue me and train me well. That help continued to be of benefit when, about seventeen months later, our son and daughter-in-law moved to where we were also. We were in close proximity again and I was happy. In retrospect, we see God needed us to move alone so we could give ourselves to the transition of the pastorate. Then, at the perfect time, when our kids needed us most, and we missed them the most, God again placed us in close proximity. It was all as God planned.

The parental journey develops and continues. As our grown kids face challenges and blessings, it has been our privilege to walk with, pray with, counsel, and help. We have laughed together, played together, vacationed together, and unfortunately, wept together. We expected the good seasons, but didn't see some of the bad seasons coming. Whether the short seasons of a job loss, or the forever tragedy of the death of our first-born grandchild, we needed to stand with our kids in ways where we were completely unprepared. But through every victory and every crushing loss, my husband and I continuously learned new parenting skills. We needed our kids in our lives, and they needed their parents in theirs.

## What I Know Now:

Just because your children mature and start the journey of their life does not mean your time of parenting is done. It just means your role changes. You may no longer spoon feed, teach to walk, help with homework, or provide a measure of forced oversight. Now your role is to pray like crazy, be available when necessary, and offer Godly advice when asked. It's a balance of invitational oversight, Biblical wisdom, and unmeasurable love. You need to give your kids enough space to make decisions and bear the responsibility for those decisions, while at the same time being a listening ear and guiding cheerleader. You cannot raise them anymore, but you will always believe in them, even when they don't believe in themselves. When asked, your good and bad experiences can be a lightened path to follow, but only if your kids will give you the permission to speak to their situation. You cannot force it, but if your love is more obvious than your words, opportunities will arise.

It is the same relationship we have with our Heavenly Father as He parents us. He speaks direction through His word, but we have the choice to follow. He never abandons us, is always available, leads but doesn't force, and our acceptance of His voice is squarely based on the foundation of His unending love. I know this isn't easy. There have been many times as a parent I wanted to keep my adult children from making foolish decisions, even when I was pretty sure they wouldn't listen. But I have noticed as they get older and I get older, our mutual love and respect grows. Even though my initial parenting skills were lacking, I tried to create an approach that was loving, accepting, and forgiving. Because of that, now I have more of a friendship with them than a parent-child relationship. Years ago, my husband and I decided to parent our kids when they were young so we could be a friend to them when they were old. We discovered it doesn't work the other way around.

Remember when the current role with your kids becomes too challenging, the enemy wants you to give up. That's particularly true when they get older and have the ability to make their own choices. It's easy to begin saying, "You are on your own, so do what you want! I don't care." But such sentiments, birthed out of your frustrations and feelings of rejection, will only create the same attitude in them. There is a war waged for the life of your children and the enemy comes to steal, kill, and destroy. Because of that attack they will *always* need someone to pray, someone available, someone who won't be critical, and someone that encourages them to believe in a God of second chances.

Look, I haven't always been the model parent. I don't know anyone who has. But I will never let my children become a ruined heap of despair and loss. Not ever! I know how to fight for them. I know how to keep inviting and praying for them to be close to the Lord. I am convinced God will give them strength to live through every season of life. I am sure the parenting invested in them when they were little will harvest a good return in their later years. And I am simple enough to trust the destiny assigned to them by their Creator will become their norm.

## Walking it Out:

The three practical things you can do as a mom:

### 1. Grow in your relationship with the Lord.

First, we must remain in daily communication with Him. We do this through reading and studying His word, thinking about what we read, and asking Him for wisdom and guidance. Next, take some time every day to pray. Don't complicate this. Just talk to the Lord. That's what prayer is...telling God what's on your mind and in your heart, good or bad. Finally, develop some friendships with other moms who are Christ followers, especially ones who are older and have walked the journey.

They not only stand with you when you need it, but can also encourage you from their personal life experiences. You might already have some Christian friends. Ask to meet with them and begin building a stronger relationship together. If you don't know anyone like that, the best place to meet this kind of friend is by regularly going to church, joining a Bible study group, joining a "Mom's Group" at your church, or finding a place to serve at your church. It's called "community" and it is an essential practice for everyone and it's of vital importance if you are a mom. Many others have blazed this motherhood path before you, and they can be the ones to help you on your journey.

## 2. Don't quit.

Motherhood isn't for sissies! Period! If you are planning to become a mom, are in the middle of the journey, or you have kids that are *supposed* to be grown-ups, you will, probably more than once, want to quit, give up, move on, hope to get fired, stay in bed, not answer the phone, or mysteriously disappear. But you can't and shouldn't. God positioned you where you are, and He will provide everything you need to succeed. Losing or walking away isn't your destiny. You are destined to the call God placed on your life, and that call is to help mold and shape the lives of another generation. That may sound ominous, but with God, ALL things are possible. ALL THINGS. We moms don't have the option to quit at any stage of our kid's development. Now go read Philippians 4:13...

## 3. Remember there is a difference between the destination and the journey.

My mom and grandmother played a big part in my life until they went to be with Jesus. I learned from these two Godly ladies that daily struggles are not my final destination, but rather just part of my journey. That means bad days and big problems are not forever. Your destiny is not one of strife and pain. Yeah, you are going to have some bad days, some very bad days. But those are only a place you travel *through*, not the place where you will always live.

Think about it this way. If you needed to drive to another city, and during your drive you hit a bunch of potholes in the road, is it okay for you to assume that wherever you drive, from that day forward, you will never find smooth pavement again? Of course not. Those holes in the road were in *that* road, not in every other road you will ever drive on. Nope! There are other parts of your journey that will be smooth and without difficulty. Pain and problems are not your destination, they are only a part of your journey.

**Do & Don't:**

- Do, on a daily basis, build a strong foundation with Him

- Don't let your relationship with the Lord stagnate

- Do stay focused on the call God has given you as a mother

- Don't give up

- Do be a part of the journey

- Don't stand by and watch

## Questions for Reflection:

1. Have you taken time to assess your relationship with your children?

   _____

   _____

   _____

   _____

2. Are you in the process of building:

   A. Good relationship with the Lord?

   B. Good relationship with your children?

   _____

   _____

   _____

   _____

3. Do you trust the Lord with your life?

_____

_____

_____

_____


4. How do you view raising your children, as a chore or blessing?

_____

_____

_____

_____


5. Do you need a new mindset? Is it a destination or journey?

_____

_____

_____

_____

## Closing Prayer:

*Thank you, Father, for giving me the opportunity to be a mom. It is a high calling, one I could never accomplish through human efforts. Thank You for always being there when I needed help, and for providing that help without judgement or criticism. You have been a great example for me in dealing with my kids. I appreciate my children and am blessed by what they have brought to my life. It's not always been fun, and not always been easy, but thank You, Lord, they developed to be fun, loving, and caring children. God, You and I have been through good times and hard times. I liked the good times better, but I'm glad that I have been able to make the motherhood journey with the children You gave me, and with You never walking away when I needed you most. It's been a good run, and I will continue to depend on your strength and wisdom to complete the mom destiny You have assigned me. You were right when You said, "I will never desert you, nor will I ever forsake you" (Hebrews 13:5) Amen!*

OTHER MOMS
NEVER TOLD ME
I COULD PROJECTILE
SQUIRT MILK OUT
MY BREASTS AS A
SUPERPOWER.

MOMMENTOR.ORG

## Chapter 9

# Other Moms Never Told Me ...
# God Can Do A Lot With a Hot Mess

*By Kami Zumwalt*

*Ruth 4:11 "All the people who were at the gate, and the elders, said, "We are witnesses. The Lord make the woman who is coming to your house like Rachel and Leah, the two who built the house of Israel."*

## I Didn't See That Coming:

*One. Hot. Mess.* We've all seen her. Standing at a park with a giant hot mocha. Sweatpants stained with eggs from breakfast. Two toddlers circling her legs like merciless, starving vultures. Messy bun. Bouncing a newborn to her chest, with lavender bags under her eyes the size of silver dollars and a glazed, "What day is it?" look on her face. Maybe, like me, you haven't just seen her in the park, you've seen her staring back at you in the mirror! If you've ever looked in the mirror and thought, "I can't remember when I've felt like such a mess." You are in good company.

Motherhood is ... messy.

*Oh my...she's beautiful and tiny and bald...and won't stop screaming!*

My first-born daughter was a tiny ball of beauty and hyper-sensitivity which would elate me in moments and terrorize me during night time feeding sessions (which happened every thirty minutes all through the night for months). This was everything I prayed for, for over four years. This tiny human was a living, breathing picture of all the dreams of pink frilly dresses and crocheted baby blankets I hoped for, plopped into my arms like a kiss from heaven.

But she was...so demanding! (They say 10 percent of babies are high need, meaning: intense, draining, unable to be satisfied, and hyperactive...also quite often gifted and brilliant!)

So, what would God do with this high octane, hand-crafted little queen in the years ahead? Dance. I knew He had shown me that much. She would be a dancer and a worshipper.

Cradling her head or admiring her dancer toes, an overwhelming quest crashed into my soul.

Perfect. I wanted to make her little dancing life...well...*perfect.*

After all, here was my chance to give her a life of peace my own childhood lacked.

Was perfection too much to ask of myself?

Of course. Most mothers put pretty high expectations on themselves. I worked hard to make perfection a reality, even in the midst of the usual messes of motherhood and a lovely but high need child. Piles of kid's clothes, blow-out diapers, sticky fingers flinging ketchup around the kitchen, screaming over car seat rides, sudden noises like the blender, and refusing to let me put her down most the day. It didn't take long to find out I was far from perfect! In fact, there were a lot of days, I felt like a complete mess!

I found out I wasn't the only one.

For some mamas, the messes go much, much deeper.

Abusive backgrounds. Painful addictions. Difficult parents. Absent parents. Depression. Dysfunctional families. For some, the mess staring back at us in the mirror can feel overwhelming. What can God do with a mom who has a messy background? A difficult upbringing? A less than perfect perception on what it means to be a mother?

A lot.

For all the moms who want to be the mom of your dreams, but your own upbringing was a bit of a nightmare, there is really good news. God has a reputation of meeting women in desperate, hot messes and building the next move of God with them.

They are all over the Bible. Desperate women in desperate situations.

## What I Know Now:

I found my own lack of perfection and days of desperation put me in good company. The bleeding woman who latched onto the fringe of Jesus' prayer shawl…a prostitute who busted down the door to a dinner she was not invited to…a widow, surrounded by the wealthy, reduced down to nothing but two measly pennies, putting the last of her possessions into an offering plate.

Jesus kept showing up and meeting them in the midst of their mess. Take Rachel and Leah's family. Marked over their household was an incredible prophetic destiny to build the entire house of Israel. I believe there is a prophetic destiny over your household as well. An assignment only your family can fulfill, and the reason your children are uniquely wired the way they are (high needs included!) Yet, if you've ever read Rachel and Leah's story, you know "dysfunctional" would be an understatement.

Picture two sisters, perhaps standing in the kitchen in the land of Haran. The older one, Leah is making bread, the younger, a shepherdess, is bringing the last of her flock down the hill for the night. The Bible describes them like this:

*Genesis 29:16-17 "Laban had two daughters: the name of the elder was Leah, and the name of the younger was Rachel. Leah's eyes were delicate, but Rachel was beautiful in form and appearance."*

The bomb-shell Rachel and the doe-eyed Leah. Like pretty much all women, there are a lot more to these sisters than meets the eye. Things might have appeared alright on the outside, but there were rumblings below the surface. (Hint. The first step to God invading our mess is to admit we have one.)

A dream man has arrived.

The cat fights aren't far away. Now, Rachel, who apparently is practically perfect...I picture her singing to sheep, strolling romantically green hillsides twenty times a day. An unforgettable shepherdess. She captured the attention of Jacob from the moment he saw her. The older, unnoticeable Leah, fades into the shadows for seven years. Jacob keeps a vow to their father, Laban, whom Jacob promised to work seven years in order to marry Rachel. The Bible says, it felt like only a few days because of the love he had for her. (Even Hallmark can't beat that one.)

Likely watching out the window for another man to miraculously show up in the dusty, desert road, no one ever comes for Leah. Overlooked. Underappreciated. Unseen. Every day, she is watching this story for her sister unfold. She's watching down the road for when her moment will arrive. After seven years, she's been waiting for her prophetic destiny.

Nothing. Not a single man in Levi's tribe. Not a single message on Facebook. No signs of anyone taking an interest in her. And understand, back then, you didn't have much of a future without a man. These days, your prophetic destiny is in Jesus, with or without a man, you have no limits to fulfilling what God has called you to. But in Haran, in the house of Laban, Leah's waiting for her own life to really begin.

So, what does her father do? Unbelievably sneaky plans envelope his heart. After the garlands of flowers and feast of the wedding night, he hides Leah in the bed chamber. In the dark of the night, Jacob sleeps with Leah, consummating his marriage to her, thinking he is with Rachel.

What a mess.

Jacob is shocked. Rachel is heartbroken. Leah is humiliated. And out of this one big dysfunctional, twisted love saga, God's about to build His Kingdom in spite of the flaws and failures of His People. These women weren't perfect. But they were available.

What would you do if you lived with another woman *and* your man? Strangling is illegal in every state, mind you. Jacob agrees to work another seven years if he can also marry

Rachel. Laban agrees. So now we have one husband. Two wives. One kitchen. One sink. One set of fine china. In one house. Lord, help us all.

## Walking it Out:

Here's what I have discovered about Leah's messes and my own:

### 1. God has a perfect match for every hot mess - tailor made

Have you ever wondered why God sewed suits for Adam and Eve in the garden? After the mess of the century, standing in guilt and unbearable shame, our great-great-great…grandparents slapped some fig leaves on and tried to hide in a funky little leaf suit in the midst of their mess. But it didn't work. Only God could clean it up, and he did so not with fig leaves, but by carefully tailoring a covering out of animal skins, to cover them completely. God is into making tailor made answers for manmade messes. He deals with us not as cookie-cutters but with unique answers to real problems.

In my own life, growing up with sexual abuse and a pretty absent father, I wanted my girls to inherit the victories I have fought for in the spirit, not the pain from my past. Just like Leah, we can work hard, and pray harder. But in order to allow God to build the next move of God through us, we will have to come face to face with a gut-wrenching word - Forgiveness.

Leah had a lot to forgive (as did Rachel for that matter). Of course, there was a beguiling father, who should have protected her. But on another level, Leah would have to forgive herself. For whatever reason, she went along with Laban's plan. Perhaps she believed whatever lies Laban may have told her, but ultimately Leah blew it too. How could she have believed Jacob would get over Rachel so easily? How could she have done such a thing to her sister?

Forgiveness is required at a deep level. We will pass our mess onto the next generation if we refuse to forgive the mistakes of the last one. When we choose to forgive, heaven will back us up and our emotions will eventually fall into line. Forgiveness does not mean what happened was okay. But it does take it out of our hands and let God be the Righteous Judge. Forgiveness is never a feeling. It is a decision. Once we say, "As an act of my will, I choose to forgive," we are on our way to healing.

Once we choose to forgive, God's hand is deployed on our behalf. And He's got a reputation of taking what the devil tried to kill you with, and turning it into your own sword. Like when David killed one giant, then years later found Goliath's sword inside the temple while Saul was chasing him. David had no weapon and a madman was after him. He goes fumbling into the temple, looking for a sword. The priest says,

"Well, we only have one...it was Goliath's."

David says, "Give it to me, there's none like it."

*Why?*

God is in the habit of taking what tried to kill you and using it for your advantage. He has a reputation of not wasting anything in your life. With one act of forgiveness you put God in a position to make the most out of a hot mess and turn it into your victory, headline story, inheritance, good, and fulfill your prophetic destiny.

## 2. Generational family messes do not have to follow you.

After the wedding, Leah must have been pretty miserable. In essence, she is a third wheel. When someone goes through profound rejection, a spirit of rejection can be overwhelming. Imagine what Leah's life was like. Jacob is still head over heels in love with her sister, and now Leah lost the hope of ever being swept off her feet by someone. She is unloved, unwanted...but she did not have to stay there. She did not have to live the rest of her life feeling abused, neglected, and ruined, and neither do we.

As a pastor, many women I've counseled with find it remarkable what God does when we simply break the power of abuse and rejection in prayer. Some have just never been told they could do so, and think because the pain was in the past, they should just move on and try to forget it. But when we specifically break the power of any abuse we endured in the name of Jesus and release the healing power of Jesus in our prayer time, change happens. We find we are not powerless, but powerful in the name of Jesus.

Leah could have lived her life in a generational cycle of curses, bitterness, and rejection and passed all of that on to her children as well. But God had other plans. *Genesis 29:31 says,* *"When the Lord saw that Leah was unloved, He opened her* *womb; but Rachel was barren."*

The enemy's plan was for Leah to live in a lifetime cycle of bareness and brokenness, but God opened her womb. I love that when we find ourselves feeling forgotten, God is looking to birth new life and creativity into our world. God says, "You feel alone? You feel unloved? You feel looked over? Let me open up a whole new place of life for you."

## 3. Decide with God's help you can make the most of a hot mess.

Leah began to have baby after baby, but you can still hear the wounds in her soul. Child after child, she tries to make up for the rejection she endured.

> *Genesis 39:32-35 "So Leah conceived and bore a* *son, and she called his name Reuben; for she said,* *"The Lord has surely looked on my affliction. Now* *therefore, my husband will love me." Then she* *conceived again and bore a son, and said, "Because* *the Lord has heard that I am unloved, He has* *therefore given me this son also." And she called his*

*name Simeon. She conceived again and bore a son, and said, "Now this time my husband will become attached to me, because I have borne him three sons." Therefore his name was called Levi. And she conceived again and bore a son, and said, "Now I will praise the Lord." Therefore she called his name Judah. Then she stopped bearing."*

And finally, she gives birth to a boy and names him, Judah. Judah means praise. *(One who extends the hand...)*

She could not find a place of significance in her ministry, relationships, marriage, or her children. She pushed and tried to make up for what was missing in her soul, but no amount of producing, accolades, or attention can give us what only God Himself can give us. Somewhere in the midst of her story, Leah finds out how to let God turn her hot mess into a hot message.

Leah hit the point of praise. Have you been there? Tired. Worn-out. Done. I have. But suddenly a praise rises out of your belly? Praise is our way out of every self-pity party the devil wants us to throw. Praise is not about perfection. Praise is real, raw, authentic. Praise isn't pretending you're all right. Praise is offering yourself to God in weariness, brokenness, and craziness and making the God who meets us in our mess bigger than it all. We speak of His beauty, and His beauty rests on us. We sing of His majesty, and the King comes in the room and lifts up our head. We honor him for His faithfulness and His faithfulness fuels us to get up and do it all again another day. Praise is not pretending we are okay. Praise is lifting our hands to God until He lifts us into His Presence and perspective.

Leah desperately needed God's perspective. She found it in praise. Perhaps she felt no one understood her pain, but God did. Praising Him was a choice. "I'm going to praise you God when I'm overlooked. I'm going to praise God even if I feel alone and unwanted. I'm going to praise You God when I can't see what You're doing, but I know it's good. I'm going to praise You God for what You've done, for what You are doing, for what You will do." *Psalm 34:1 says, "Your praise shall continually be in my mouth."*

Our Maker makes the most out of every mistake, every moment, and out of you and me. Out of Leah's hot mess, God makes the most of it. You recall the genealogy of Jesus Christ? Look what He did with Leah's life.

*Matthew 1:1-6 "The genealogy of Jesus. Abraham begot Isaac, Isaac begot Jacob, and Jacob begot Judah and his brothers. Judah begot Perez and Zerah by Tamar, Perez begot Hezron, and Hezron begot Ram. Ram begot Amminadab, Amminadab begot Nahshon, and Nahshon begot Salmon. Salmon begot Boaz by Rahab, Boaz begot Obed by Ruth, Obed begot Jesse, and Jesse begot David the king.... And Jacob begot Joseph the husband of Mary, of whom was born Jesus who is called Christ."*

Leah, Rachel, and their two maids, Bilhah and Zilpah, birthed the twelve tribes of Israel. A nation filled with the glory of prophets, priests, and kings. None of them were perfect mothers. Leah had Reuban, Simeon, Levi and Judah. Rachel, desperate for children, gave her maid, Bilhah, to Jacob and she birthed Dan and Naphtali. Leah then asked Jacob to take her own maid, Zilpah, and had Gad and Asher. Leah went on then to have three more children; Issachar, Zebulun and one girl, Dinah (Genesis 30).

This is the family God wove His story of redemption through! Out of all the brothers God could have used to be the blood line for King David, and ultimately the Messiah, He chose the tribe of Judah. Leah's son. From the woman who was unloved, unwanted, overlooked, forgotten, second class, second rate, and *far* from perfect, yet chose to praise God, came the answer to all of humanity.

In the absence of perfection these women still brought about God's purposes.

Hidden inside your home are callings, giftings, graces, anointings, and assignments to advance the Kingdom of God and He's not looking to see if you are perfect. He's looking to see if you are available to be a vessel in His hands. He's not looking at your past to see if you qualify for the next move of God. He's looking for women who will say yes to the destiny God has woven into their family line.

If you have a broken past, God still has a whole and glorious future planned for you and your children's children. Walking through my backyard one day, pondering on how good God really is, He spoke a word to me I believe is His heart for mamas with difficult upbringings everywhere. "You can give them the childhood I wanted you to have..."

## Questions for Reflection:

1. What can God produce from your life? *What can God make out of the situations when we have felt unloved, or overlooked?*

_____

_____

_____

_____

2. What is God working to birth into the world through you? *How may God change the course of generations from one woman who will lift up her hands?*

_____

_____

_____

_____

3. How can you shift your focus to how much God has always wanted you? *Especially for those who have often felt unwanted or unloved growing up.*

_____

_____

_____

_____

4. Do you expect your kids to deal with the same issues your family has? *Have you broken the power of those things in prayer and declared God's Word over them instead?*

_____

_____

_____

_____

5. Are you aware of how your day to day life is connected to the eternal destinies of others? *He is the God who makes the most out of every moment. He's the God who makes the most out of every misery. He is the one who makes the most out of you and me. Was Leah aware her day-to-day tasks mattered? That her decision to praise*

*while flipping pancakes or enduring another day of feeling unwanted would affect generations to come?*

_____

_____

_____

_____

## Closing Prayer:

*Father, thank You for making me into a forerunner in my family. Thank You for the prophetic destiny You have declared over my household. I embrace the call and assignment You have given to us, and in Jesus name I break the power of abuse, neglect, rejection, sorrow, shame, and depression off myself and my children. I break the power of every generational curse off our home. And I agree with Your Word, and say In Jesus Name, we are blessed, healed, forgiven, and free in the mighty name of Jesus.*

# OTHER MOMS NEVER TOLD ME HOW MUCH I WOULD GROW TO HATE STICKERS.

Chapter 10

# Other Moms Never Told Me ...
## You Were Made For This

*By Christi Stone*

*"It is not that we think we are qualified to do*

*anything on our own. Our qualification comes from*

*God."*

*2 Corinthians 3:5*

## I Didn't See That Coming:

Recently, I looked through "old" photos of my children. I cried. I laughed. Shocked at some of my hairstyles and outfit styles I chose, I thought to myself, *"Who was that girl, y'all? And where were my friends to help a sister out?"* But mostly, I saw a young mom who had no idea what she was headed into and what she could do if she only knew she was made for this.

I am a mother to six children, three biological and three non-biological. I also have two spiritual daughters and four grand babes. Life is FUN! But it wasn't always that way. Going from a married mom of three, to a single mom of three, to a mom of six, and then to a mom of eight with four grand babes is a journey. A blessed one, but a journey, nonetheless. It comes with its trials, with its lessons, with its laughter, and with plenty of love and forgiveness.

Y'all, being a mom is hard, but you were made for this. You can do this. No matter the season, no matter the age, you will never stop being made for this.

As a mama, I have so many stories I could tell from wiping little behinds, to teenage years, to sending a child off to college, to becoming a military mom, to becoming a Nana. Everything from choir concerts and baseball games to hospital admissions and court battles. One of my favorite stories to tell is this one...

When I met my husband, Shane, I knew instantly he was the one. I knew God hand picked him just for me. But it wasn't just him that God handpicked. He handpicked Brandon, Aaron, and Isabella, and then later Lauren, Jody, and grand babes, Cam, Josie, and twins Kason and Keaton. Becoming a mom to that many kids that fast, over a period of three years, was insane to me. Why? Because I wasn't supposed to be a mom at all.

At age 15, I was diagnosed with PCOS, a condition involving the ovaries which is one of the leading causes of infertility in women. I was told I would never have kids naturally. After three high risk pregnancies and (praise God) three kids later, I had a painful hysterectomy, and then a divorce. I again believed I would never have any more children, and maybe wasn't meant for this. I was told (and believed) the lie that I wasn't a good mom, that I had failed my kids. Anyone else ever had a family member disapprove of your parenting? I believed the lie, if others thought this, then surely God must too.

Have you ever felt that way? Have you ever felt no matter what you do, it's not right? Have you ever found yourself in situations or seasons you have no idea how to navigate? Have you ever wondered what God was thinking when He made you a mom? Me too, sister. Me too. I had to learn how to be the one thing I thought I was never meant to be, and it was terrifying. I felt like if there was anything certain, it was I would not win any "mother of the year" awards.

But here's the truth, I was made for this, and so are you. It doesn't matter what the world says you aren't, what your family says, what your friends say, even what you say. The truth is, you were made for this and for them. You are the one God chose to guide them, teach them, learn with them, nurture them, be grace for them, and them for you. Because, it isn't what *you are not,* it's who *you are,* that God saw when He made you for this. The world told me I was a terrible mom of 3, and then God gave me 5 more.

One of the scariest seasons for me was becoming a dreaded "stepmom." I had zero clue how to navigate this season of change, much less with teens and pre-teens. Teenagers are scary enough when you have known them their entire life, but how do you "mom" kids that clearly didn't ask for you to be in their life? How do you show equal love to both the kids you came with and the kids you've gained? How do you be the mom to everyone and do it well? How do you navigate love and hurt all at the same time? How do you set a standard of culture in a season where you feel you have no influence? How do you "blend"? I had so many questions, but I knew one thing, I was gonna give it my best and I was gonna trust God knew what He was doing.

In the following, I will share what I've learned while becoming a mom to many during a season of criticism, not only from others, but from myself.

## What I Know Now:

Hindsight is 20/20. Isn't that what they say? Have you ever heard, or maybe even have said, "If only I would have known then what I know now?" Yes and amen. Me too girl, me too. The one amazing thing about having kids that range from 27-12 is hopefully by the time my little guy goes through it, I've learned a thing or two. But reality is, every kid is different, and the same situation requires a different means of navigation. Here are some of the things I've learned through my seasons of trying to remember I was made for this.

Criticism will never weigh more than truth. Truth is, you were chosen. Just as Mary was chosen to carry Jesus, both in her heart and in her womb. You were chosen. I picture Mary on a dirt road minding her own business in an uneventful life and BOOM...life changes not only for her, but for everyone, for the rest of history. Talk about pressure. I often think of how she navigated the criticism that was sure to come. How did she react? Did she sweat and pace? Did she stay calm? Did she have a holy moment or a holy cow moment? Let's be real and remember *she was human* and most likely a teenager! But here's what she knew...

No matter the criticism, no matter what, she would say, "yes" even if she needed the journey to show her she was made for this. And so do we. I love the passage in Luke 1:28-41 where Jesus' birth is announced to Mary. This passage has three different particular phrases I relate with, and I think you will too.

> *"Gabriel appeared to her and said, "Grace to you, young woman, for the Lord is with you and so you are anointed with great favor." Mary was deeply troubled over the words of the angel and bewildered over what this may mean for her. But the angel reassured her, saying, "Do not yield to your fear, Mary, for the Lord has found delight in you and has chosen to surprise you with a wonderful gift. He will be supreme and will be known as the Son of the Highest. And the Lord God will enthrone him as King on his ancestor David's throne."*

> *Mary said, "But how could this happen? I am still a virgin!" Gabriel answered, "The Spirit of Holiness*

*will fall upon you and almighty God will spread his*
*shadow of power over you in a cloud of glory! This*
*is why the child born to you will be holy, and he*
*will be called the Son of God. What's more, your*
*aged aunt, Elizabeth, has also become pregnant*
*with a son. The 'barren one' is now in her sixth*
*month. Then Mary responded, saying, "This is*
*amazing! I will be a mother for the Lord! As his*
*servant, I accept whatever he has for me. May*
*everything you have told me come to pass." And the*
*angel left her."*

*Luke 1:28-30, 32, 34-36, 38 (TPT)*

The first part I relate with and love so much is it says Mary was "deeply troubled." Were you scared or nervous when you found out you were becoming a mom? I remember exactly where I was and what I was doing when I found out I was about to give birth. I also remember exactly what I felt when I was about to become a mom to *many*. I was "deeply troubled," meaning scared to death. It can definitely be scary to do something so big you know others will never believe you. Becoming and being a mom can be scary like that. Whether you are raising natural children, step-children, or adopted children, being a mom can sometimes cause us to be "deeply troubled." But just like Mary, you are highly favored and He has chosen you just like He chose her.

The second point in the passage I love is the part where she says "yes" to the promise of Jesus that God is offering to her. I often overlook this. Wow, what an honor. But as there was great honor, there was great opportunity. Opportunity for obedience and to step into something greater. We have that ability as moms. We have the ability to partner with God in saying "yes," not only to the responsibility of the children He is giving us, but to the promise that it holds. Mary did not conceive naturally, and for some of us, neither did we. But it didn't change that she was made for this, and so are we.

*In Luke 1:41, it says "At the moment she heard Mary's voice, the baby within Elizabeth's womb jumped and kicked. And suddenly, Elizabeth was filled to overflowing with the Holy Spirit!"*

The first person to recognize Jesus was another baby. I am wrecked by this thought. Another child. Another child in the womb. It shows me, no matter what, no matter when, no matter how, God is in the relation. Whether we are born into a natural family, if we are "blended" through marriage, adopted, or through spiritual connection, God is in the relation. I believe that same anointing is in our families, that God wants each of us to experience the "leaping" of our children, and I believe we only experience that through our children and our experiences with them. Families were never designed to be perfect. They were designed to be relational. Truth is, as moms we are always going to have a season to be in. Are we tuned in to the "leaping" the Lord wants to do in us through our children?

I have learned through the criticism, the pain, and the heartache of being a mom at times, I love the leaping. I love saying "yes" to God. I love watching Him in the relations I have with my kids, and in relations they have with each other. I love finding the uniqueness of each child, and loving them from that place. I love knowing, like Mary, I was hand-picked and highly favored to parent my children.

I always love to hear different perspectives on parenting, on being a mom. But I don't always know how to apply it. Here's a few tips I have found that have worked in our house.

## Walking It Out:

### 1. Take a time out.

This is crucial for all of us. A time out can look like, and be different, for every mom depending on the circumstances of your household. My kids have been given authority over my timeouts. Many times I do not think I need one, or have time for one, and they will remind me that, in fact, I do. A time out resets, refreshes, and renews where we are and what we want to accomplish. It refocuses what the end result needs to look like. It may or may not change the route we take, but it most definitely will redirect our perspective. When dealing with multiple kids, in and out of critical seasons, time outs will always be needed. For me, a time out looks like quiet time in my closet with coffee. The closet is the only place my kids don't look for me. It's the perfect place for a time of prayer and for griping to Jesus about why I am right. And it's also the most perfect place to receive His grace for when I realize I am not always right.

## 2. Remember you are only one person and God has never intended you to do this mom thing alone.

Find your tribe and lean on them. Community is so important when raising our kids. You have heard the saying, "it takes a village," well, this sister needs a state in some seasons. Community allows us to learn and explore new ways of relating to our kids. A few friends and I have a walkie talkie style video chat we do most every day, talking about everything from laundry to homework to losing our ever-loving minds. It's a safe place to vent, to pray, to have accountability, and to breathe. Find your tribe and let them love you hard. If you need a tribe, Jesus and I got you.

## 3. Never be afraid to admit to being less than perfect

I have learned, relearned, and continue to learn this lesson. So many times as moms we believe our kids need to see our perfection when, in reality, they just crave our participation. When I began participating and leaving the perfection to God, the weight of the world was lifted. So what, if I gave the wrong sandwich to the wrong kid? So what, if the dishes sat while I played Uno with them? So what, if I called them by their sibling's name? So what! When we put down the never ending, exhausting task of being perfect, it allows us to participate. To participate in their dreams, in their questions, in their struggles, and in their successes. When we participate, I can only imagine the "leaping" we will feel as we remember we were made for this, and for them.

## Questions for Reflection:

1. What is one thing you love about being a mom? This is so important to help us remember we were made for this.

   _____

   _____

   _____

   _____

2. What criticism have you endured, and have you allowed God to access it? We will all endure criticism, but when we give it to God, we see His truth about us will always be bigger.

   _____

   _____

   _____

   _____

3. When was the last time you felt the "leaping" from your children like Elizabeth felt? May we all slow down and take the time to feel the "leaping" from the

spirit Elizabeth felt. May we look at our children and see Jesus in and through them.

_____

_____

_____

_____

4. What are you saying, "Yes" to? May we all partner with God and His promise in our lives as mamas.

_____

_____

_____

_____

5. Are you participating or performing? May we all realize when we are in a spirit of performance and return to participating with our kids. They don't need our perfection. They just need us.

_____

_____

_____

_____

## Closing Prayer:

*Jesus, thank You for the opportunity to serve the kingdom by serving my children. Help me on the good days, the bad days, the mundane days, and the crazy days, to remember I was made for this. Help me to walk in my favor and to acknowledge I am chosen. I do not lack. I do not fail. I am abundant and I learn. May I always remember Your grace is sufficient and I was made for this. In Jesus name, amen.*

# Endnotes

[i] Wilder, J. (2004). *The Complete Guide to Living with Men.* Shepherd's House, Inc.

[ii] Middleton, K. (2020, February 15). *The Duchess of Cambridge on the early years.* Retrieved from Happy Baby, Happy Mum: https://play.acast.com/s/happymumhappybaby/theduchessofcambrid geontheearlyyears

iii. Underwood, C. (2020). "Put Yourself FIrst" Commercial. CALIA.

[iv] Evans, T. (2019). *The Tony Evans Bible Commentary.* Nashville: Holman Bible Publishers.

[v] Lewis, C. (1960, 2017). *The Four Loves.* San Francisco : Harper One.

38936207R00128